High Level Synthesis of Pipelined Datapaths

High Level Synthesis of Pipelined Datapaths

Péter Arató
Tamás Visegrády
István Jankovits
Technical University of Budapest, Hungary

JOHN WILEY & SONS, LTD
Chichester · New York · Weinheim · Brisbane · Singapore · Toronto

Copyright © 2001 Panem Limited, Budapest, Hungary

Published by   John Wiley & Sons, Ltd
                Baffins Lane, Chichester
                West Sussex, PO19 1UD, England

                National 01243 779777
                International (+44) 1243 779777
e-mail (for orders and customer service enquiries): cs-books@wiley.co.uk

Visit our Home Page on http://www.wiley.co.uk or http://www.wiley.com

Other Wiley Editorial Offices

John Wiley & Sons, Inc., 605 Third Avenue,
New York, NY 10158-0012, USA

Wiley-VCH Verlag GmbH
Pappelallee 3, D-69469 Weinheim, Germany

John Wiley Australia Ltd, 33 Park Road, Milton,
Queensland 4064, Australia

John Wiley & Sons (Canada) Ltd, 22 Worcester Road
Rexdale, Ontario, M9W 1L1, Canada

John Wiley & Sons (Asia) Pte Ltd, 2 Clementi Loop #02-01,
Jin Xing Distripark, Singapore 129809

Library of Congress Cataloging-in-Publication Data

Arató, Péter
   High level synthesis of pipelined datapaths / . Péter Arató, Tamás Visegrády, István Jankovits
      p. cm.
   Includes bibliographical references and index.
   ISBN 0 471 49582 4
      1.   Computer architecture 2. Computers, Pipeline. I. Visegrády, Tamás. II. Jankovits,
   István. III. Title

   QA76.9. A73 A68 2001
   004.2'2—dc21   00-054086

British Library Cataloguing in Publication Data

A catalogue record for this book is available from the British Library

ISBN 0 47149582 4

Produced from LaTeX files supplied by the authors
Printed and bound in Great Britain by Biddles Ltd., Guildford and Kings Lynn
This book is printed on acid-free paper responsibly manufactured from sustainable forestry,
in which at least two trees are planted for each one used for paper production.

Contents

Preface

The continuous fast development of the semiconductor industry offers system designers more and more complex functional units as building blocks to be applied as ready-made components with *intellectual property (IP)*. The adaptability, programmability, and reconfigurability of such components (IPs) provide flexibility in *reusing* the same types of them. In this way, time to market can essentially be reduced, since testing and rapid prototyping require less effort. However, the more or less exact design methodology of logic synthesis based on simple building blocks (gates, flip-flops, registers, counters, etc.) has to be radically reformed. The system specification based on the problem to be solved can no longer be performed by considering the specific building blocks as physical resources. Much higher level of abstraction is needed for starting the design procedure called *system-level synthesis (SLS)* in this case, in order to make use of increasing complexity of the components in the optimization [Bor00]. This higher abstraction level is called *behavioural specification* of the system and it involves fictive behavioural components. The later steps of system-level synthesis yield a proper decomposition into the real complex components (IPs) including their control and communication. The IP vendors provide a growing variety of products specified in catalogues, also on a behavioural level, and there are also fully programmable processors among them. Therefore, system-level synthesis may result in an architecture which consists of both hardware and software components. In other words, the so-called *hardware-software codesign* principles are inherent parts of system-level synthesis.

The most crucial steps in system-level synthesis are the special decomposition algorithms constructing an architecture from predefined IPs and the communication between them. The requirements on speed, total cost and communication cost, complexity of control, etc. set strict conditions on the decomposition algorithms and IP selection. The *design automation* has a great importance also in system-level synthesis, because most of the design steps have an NP-hard character and decisions made by trial and heuristics are not always avoidable. The recent development in this field makes it possible to produce more and more complex systems on a single chip *(System-on-Chip, SoC)* by top-down methodology starting from a high abstraction level of behavioural specification. This high-level specification is based generally on high-level description languages providing a proper input to the design automation tools.

The first attempts to start the design from a behavioural level were the so-called *high-level synthesis (HLS)* approaches in the mid eighties. Basically, the optimization of the digital signal processing chips as special-purpose hardware structures has been supported by the HLS algorithms. The real hardware resources as components were already complex enough (but not so complex as IPs today and in the future) for handling their capabilities on a behavioural level as a composition from fictive elementary operations. The main principles of HLS can be extended and applied also in SLS. HLS algorithms may be used beneficially in the design of IPs as well. The speed requirements need pipeline data processing function for many application fields. Therefore, the HLS algorithms should be able to support the optimization of structures functioning in pipeline mode. An important part of the new design methodology is the set of high-level synthesis algorithms for the pipelined datapaths of hardware components.

In this book, models and methods are presented for solving this high-level synthesis problem, but a complete overview of the state-of-the-art has not been aimed. There are many excellent works in the field, which present the state-of-the-art on a high didactic and technical level (see Further Reading). It would not be easy and worthy to compete with them. The approach presented in this book is based on the authors' research results at the Department of Control Engineering and Information Technology, Technical University of Budapest. In this sense, the book may be considered as a research report and a university textbook at the same time. The material has been used in special courses of the Electrical Engineering curriculum at the Technical University of Budapest for four years. As well as introducing the basic algorithms for data dominated structures (scheduling, allocation, buffer insertion, replication of operations, synchronization), control principles and a unique handling of multiple-process recursive loops are also described. A tutorial computer aided design tool (PIPE) developed by the authors is presented which starts from a behavioural elementary operation graph specification and yields an allocated structural description of the pipelined datapath. The usage of PIPE and the evaluation of the algorithms are illustrated on benchmark problems.

The book offers a didactic step-by-step treatment of the subject using simple examples for explaining the rather complicated topics of basically NP-hard problems. The book is recommended not only for graduate and postgraduate students studying or researching high-level synthesis or related topics, but also for engineers and researchers, who are familiar or would like to become familiar with the subject.

The research work of the authors has been supported by the grants OTKA T17236, OTKA T030178, COPERNICUS CP940453, FKFP 0416/97 at the Department of Control Engineering and Information Technology, Technical University of Budapest. The authors express special thanks to Prof. Dr. Béla Fehér for his valuable and competent work in reviewing the original version of the manuscript published by Panem, Budapest, 1999. His comments and suggestions for modification improved the presentation considerably.

The authors are very grateful to Tibor Kandár and Zoltán Mohr for their contribution as PhD students in solving benchmarks and completing the final form of the manuscript.

Budapest, 30 September 2000.

Péter Arató
Tamás Visegrády
István Jankovits

List of Figures

List of Tables

1

Introduction

The high-speed digital signal processing and most real-time applications require *special-purpose hardware units (Application-Specific Integrated Circuits, ASICs)* executing a special task or being able to solve a limited but rather complex problem set. Due to the technological development, the size and the price of such units are being reduced but the speed requirements and the complexity of the executable tasks are increasing. The functional parts of the units are the *datapath* consisting of *processors* and *data connections* between them and the *control part* coordinating the data path. One of the ways of increasing the processing speed is *pipelining* that introduces new input data before obtaining the results for the previous calculations. The frequency of the data introduction expresses how often the unit is restarted with new input data. This *restarting period* determines the *throughput* of the unit. The longest time between the introduction of an input data and receiving the result calculated on it is called the *latency* of the unit. Reducing the restarting period may cause a longer latency, since some of the methods used in this step introduce *buffers* (delay effects) into the data path.

Based on the problem to be solved by the special-purpose unit, defining the processors, the data connections and the control part under several constraints (speed, cost, size, technology, etc.) is the *structure design*. There are many commercial computer-aided design (CAD) tools (VIEWLOGIC, LOG/IC, ABEL, XILINX, CADENCE, etc.) starting with the structure as input and yielding a complete documentation for fabricating the unit (layout for VLSI ASIC, FPGA programs, etc.). In most cases, the input of these tools is a register transfer level *(RTL)* description of the structure. Among the RTL structural descriptive languages, VHDL is the most widely used and standardized, which can be applied not only for structural but also for behavioural and gate level description. The procedure from the structural description to the realization in silicon is called *silicon compilation* and can be executed by commercial CAD tools called *silicon compilers*.

Obviously many different structures can be designed for a given task or problem set to be solved. Designing an advantageous structure for silicon compilation is called *high-level synthesis (HLS)* which starts with a specification of the problem to be solved by the unit and provides the RTL description of the structure. Based on the initial specification, a *behavioural description* is generated at first, which refers to fictive *elementary operations* of the problem to be solved. There are many variations of splitting a problem into elementary operations, therefore the effectiveness of the HLS procedure is strongly influenced by this step. Unfortunately, the optimal behavioural description as a decomposition cannot be generated without trials and heuristics. The most advantageous formal specification of the behavioural prescription is a *dataflow-like representation*, which is easy to be described also by behavioural level VHDL [IEE88]. The next step of the HLS is to *schedule* and *synchronize* the elementary operations by a proper control in order to fulfil the throughput requirements without violating other constraints (available building blocks as hardware resources, technology, etc.). Based on a schedule, the processors can be specified by constructing proper subsets of elementary operations that may be executed by the same processor. This step of the HLS is called *allocation*, which covers the elementary operations, by a set of real processors already representing the structural design. The allocation constraints may require identical elementary operations in the same processors, a limited complexity of the processors, or a regular structure (systolic array), etc. Each of these constraints may need different schedules for a beneficial structure. Therefore, the scheduling and the allocation steps are not independent of each other, and trials and heuristics could not be avoided for finding an optimal solution. Each step of the HLS involves NP-hard problems. In this sense, no systematic method can be formulated for a global optimum in the HLS. However, there exist many heuristic and iterative methods for finding locally optimal or simply beneficial solutions in the steps of the HLS separately. These HLS methods are very important and efficient, since they usually yield a more advantageous structure for the silicon compilation than a structure defined by intuition. Having defined the structure, almost all the freedom of the behavioural description is lost. The HLS methods are dedicated to control this freedom decreasing step by step in order to provide a beneficial structure for the further design phases [Cam90, CR89, PP86, MR92, IEE93].

Based on the above considerations, Figure 1 illustrates the main steps of HLS.

In this book, models and methods are presented for high-level logic synthesis of pipelined structures. The problem to be solved by the structure is initially split into theoretical elementary operations with arbitrary duration times. The behavioural description of this system is based on a special synchronized data flow-like representation, which provides an easy way to formulate the

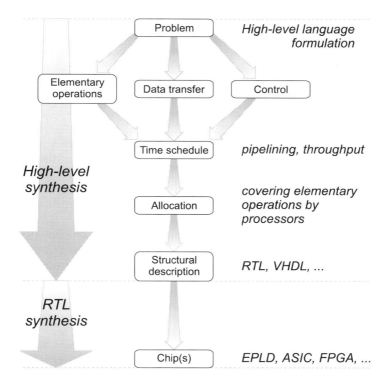

Figure 1   The main steps of high-level synthesis

scheduling and allocation steps of the methods. In the basic method, the pipeline mode needs no extra efforts, and the method ensures a restarting period, which can be given in advance. The mobility and scheduling of the theoretical elementary operations are represented by inserting extra buffer registers into the dataflow-like data path and a structural pipelining can be established by applying extra copies of some operations. The minimal number of buffers to be inserted, the optimal selection of the operational units to be applied in multiple copies and the minimal number of the required copies are the main goals in the first design phase [ABR+94]. Based on these results, the second part of the method provides a solution to the resource allocation problem. It is proven that the concurrence of two elementary operations can be considered as a compatibility relation between them. Thus, a proper cover of the non-concurrent operations can represent the hardware resources, i.e. the real processors. Calculating the cover, several constraints for the types of processors and the data path structure can be taken into consideration [AB96, Lip91].

Besides the basic model and method, the well-known HLS methods (list scheduling, force-directed scheduling, and ILP method) are also presented based on the most relevant references in that field.

The main principles of the latest development in the field towards hardware-software codesign and system-level synthesis are outlined in a separate chapter.

The usage of a HLS CAD software tool is illustrated on *standard benchmarks* and the accompanying CD-ROM with the tool serves for exercising and solving other problems besides benchmarks.

The content of this book can be considered specific in comparison with the relevant approaches in the literature in the following sense:

1. The algorithms always handle pipeline mode (non-pipeline is treated as the special case of pipeline), and the desired restarting period can be given in advance.

2. The behavioural datapath model is a special synchronous dataflow-like elementary operation graph, which helps in avoiding hazards during the design steps starting after high-level synthesis.

3. The data synchronizing algorithm provides directly the ASAP or ALAP schedule by inserting delay effects into the datapath. Any other schedule can be obtained by moving the delay effects as fictive buffer registers along the data lines.

4. The desired predefined restarting period can be achieved by inserting the minimal number of buffer registers and/or applying the minimal number of copies of replicated (multiple or structurally pipelined) operations.

5. The algorithms are extended to multiple-process recursive loops.

6. The allocation algorithm is based on a generic handling of pair-wise non-concurrence of operations as a compatibility relation.

2

The Elementary Operation Graph (EOG)

The problem to be solved can be considered as a sequence of elementary operations between the input $(x_1, \ldots, x_n)$ and the output data $(y_1, \ldots, y_m)$. Data connections and elementary operations represent a principal data path for the problem to be solved. The control of this principal data path can be imagined as a centralized counter or simple distributed handshake units (shown later). The pipeline scheduling and allocation are accomplished on the principal data path and the resulting structure also involves the control specification. The principal data path is assumed to be synchronized by a clock signal, which also influences the elementary operations, i.e. the *duration* or *execution time* is specified by the number of the clock periods between the beginning and the end of the operation.

A simple graph representation of the principal data path is illustrated in Figure 2 for the basic cell of a fast Fourier-transformation algorithm as the problem to be solved. Applying the notation of Figure 2(d) the numbers at the inputs of the elementary operations e_i of the EOG refer to the points of time, at which the first data arrive on these inputs. For example, $v_{2,1} = 10$ on the left input of e_2, because the first data arrives from e_1 in the 10th clock cycle. In this case, e_1 is the predecessor of e_2 (in notation: $e_1 \rightarrow e_2$) and $t_1 = 10$ implies that e_1 provides its first output in the 10th clock cycle. The elementary operations of the EOG are assumed to have a dataflow-like character with assumptions as follows:

1. e_i is started only after having finished every e_j, for which $e_j \rightarrow e_i$ holds.

2. e_i requires all its input data during the whole duration time t_i.

3. e_i may change its output during the whole duration time t_i.

4. e_i holds its actual output stable until its next start.

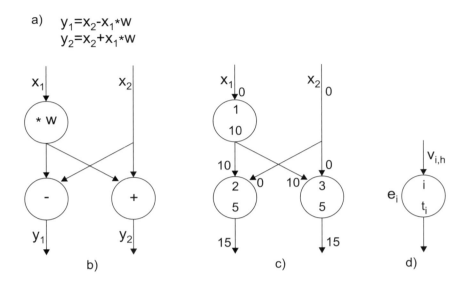

a) $y_1 = x_2 - x_1 * w$
$y_2 = x_2 + x_1 * w$

Figure 2   a) The problem to be solved. b) A data-flow representation.
c) The Elementary Operation Graph (EOG). d) Notations for EOG

Assumption 1 expresses the data dependence in EOG. Assumptions 2, 3 and 4 are made for avoiding data buffers between each pair of operations and for making the hazard elimination easier at the realization stage.

For the sake of simplicity, each e_i in the EOG (each node) may have only one output data (leaving edge) and at most two input data (arriving edge) except the conditional branches (shown later). If the output supplies several inputs, then several edges may represent the same single output.

The latest output of the whole EOG determines the latency *(L)* of the principal data path. In Figure 2(c), $L = 15$. In a pipeline mode, the second input data of the EOG is introduced earlier than L. In this way, the cyclic restarting with new input data occurs more frequently than the period determined by L. The pipeline mode means that the *restarting period (R)* is shorter than L. Thus, the throughput for input data sequences can be increased depending on the value of R. It is obvious that there are some limitations for decreasing the value of R, because the duration times of the operations in the EOG and the data connections strongly influence the earliest acceptance of the new data. In the next chapters, a method will be presented for achieving a desired restarting period by some modifications of the EOG.

3

Reducing the restarting period

3.1 Inserting buffers

Let it be assumed that the EOG does not contain loops. In this case, the EOG can be considered as a simple assembly of independent sequences of operations starting with an operation at the input of the EOG and ending with an operation at the output of the EOG. Let these sequences be called *transfer sequences* (TS).

The EOG in Figure 2 involves the TSs, as follows:

$$S_{1,1} = e_1, e_2, e_3$$
$$S_{1,2} = e_1, e_2, e_5, e_6, e_7$$
$$S_{4,1} = e_4, e_5, e_6, e_7$$

or with a simplified notation:

$$S_{1,1} = 1, 2, 3$$
$$S_{1,2} = 1, 2, 5, 6, 7$$
$$S_{4,1} = 4, 5, 6, 7$$

The notation $S_{i,k}$ means the kth TS beginning with e_i.

Each $S_{i,k}$ involves a sequence of duration times $D_{i,k}$. For example, $D_{4,1}$ belongs to $S_{4,1}$:

$$D_{4,1} = t_4, t_5, t_6, t_7$$

or simply

$$D_{4,1} = 4, 2, 3, 2$$

If $e_i \rightarrow e_j$, then according to assumptions 2 and 3 in the previous chapter, e_i must not be restarted with new input data more frequently than the time period t_i+t_j allows it. Otherwise, e_j could not receive stable input data during its whole duration time. Thus, e_i can be considered in a busy state during a time domain with the length of $q_i = t_i + t_j$. In Figure 3, the values of q_i are given on the left side of the nodes. Note that q_2 has two different values depending on the successor operations e_3 or e_5, and for the e_is driving directly the outputs of the EOG, $t_j = 0$ is considered. Thus, to each $S_{i,k}$, a busy time sequence $Q_{i,k}$ can be ordered. For example:

$$Q_{1,1} = q_1, q_2, q_3 \quad \text{i.e.} \quad 5, 8, 5$$
$$Q_{1,2} = q_1, q_2, q_5, q_6, q_7 \quad \text{i.e.} \quad 5, 5, 5, 5, 2,$$

where q_2 occurs with different values depending on the TS.

Note that e_5 must not be started with the first data earlier than the 5th clock cycle (Assumption 1). Therefore, the busy time of e_4 should have been calculated as $t_i + 1 + t_j$, because $v_{5,3} - v_{5,4} = 1$ holds in this case. For the sake of simplicity, the influence of such interactions between transfer sequences will be neglected for the time being. This problem is detailed in Chapter 4 dealing with synchronization.

If each $S_{i,k}$ is considered separately, then the above constraints do not allow to restart it in shorter time periods than the maximal value in $Q_{i,k}$. In this sense, the shortest restarting period $\min R_{i,k}$ of $S_{i,k}$ can be expressed:

$$R_{i,k} \geq \max Q_{i,k} + 1$$
$$\min R_{i,k} = \max Q_{i,k} + 1,$$

where $+1$ stands for an extra clock cycle to properly separate the restarting periods. This additional safety can eliminate all transient errors or hazards caused by coincidence of edges in subsequent restarting periods. In other words, assuming the extra clock cycle, many realization problems need not be taken into consideration during the high-level synthesis stage of the design. The only disadvantage of this solution is the speed loss caused by the extra clock cycle between restarting periods. However, this assumption helps in hazard elimination at the realization stage. Omitting $+1$ would not hurt the validity and the generality of the further calculations, as the most practical methods in the literature (shown later) do it. Based on the above considerations, the extra safety clock cycle will be added in the further calculations.

According to Figure 3:

$$\min R_{1,1} = 9$$
$$\min R_{1,2} = 6$$
$$\min R_{4,1} = 7$$

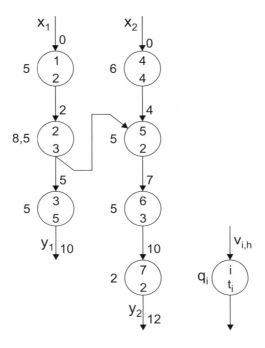

Figure 3 Elementary operation graph for illustrating the transfer and
busy time sequences

It is trivial that the minimal restarting period for the whole EOG is:

$$\min R = \max\left(\min R_{i,k}\right) = \max\left(\max Q_{i,k} + 1\right).$$

In Figure 3:

$$\min R = 9$$

To reduce the value of $\min R$, additional buffer registers may be inserted
into the EOG. The principle of the method is illustrated on a section of a TS
in Figure 4. By inserting a buffer register as an additional special operation
e_p with $t_p = 1$, the busy time of e_h can be reduced if $t_j > 1$. Let it be assumed
that $\max\left(Q_{i,k}\right) = q_h$ and $t_h > 1$ and $t_j > 1$ hold before inserting the buffer.
In this case, $q'_h < q_h$ holds after the insertion of the buffer and so the modified
value of $\min R_{i,k}$ can be smaller than it was originally. This way of reducing
the restarting period by inserting a buffer after e_h cannot be effective any more
if $\max\left(Q_{i,k}\right) = t_h + 1$ has already been achieved. If e_h has no successor i.e. it
produces one of the outputs of the whole EOG, then $q_h = t_h$ is interpreted,

and so the buffer insertion after e_h has no sense. Thus, the minimal value of the restarting period obtainable by buffer insertion is:

$$\min R = \max \left(\max D_{i,k} + 2\right),$$

if the operation with maximal duration has successor. Otherwise:

$$\min R = \max \left(\max D_{i,k} + 1\right).$$

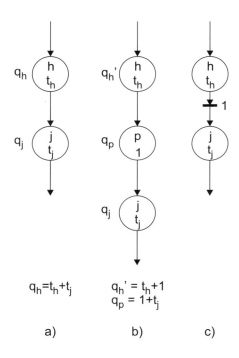

$$q_h = t_h + t_j \qquad q_h{}' = t_h + 1$$
$$q_p = 1 + t_j$$

a)   b)   c)

Figure 4   a) A section of a transfer sequence. b) The new busy times after inserting the extra buffer register. c) A symbolic notation for the buffer register inserted additionally for reducing the restarting period

To achieve a given restarting period $R > \min R$, a buffer register is required after each e_h having a busy time q_h greater than $R - 1$ and having a duration time for which $R < t_h + 2$ does not hold. If this inequality holds, then the buffer insertion is not effective, since the desired R cannot be achieved in such a way. If e_h has no successor operation (it supplies the output of the EOG), then the buffer insertion does not make sense and the inequality $R < t_h + 1$ represents the case in which the desired R cannot be achieved [AB96]. Obviously, $t_h = 1$ also excludes the buffer insertion, even if the other conditions are met. In Figure 5, the only necessary buffer insertion for the EOG in Figure 3 is illustrated providing $\min R = 5 + 2 = 7$. It is trivial that the latency of the EOG may increase as a consequence of inserting buffers, but this is not the case in Figure 5, since the latency is determined by the longest transfer sequence, i.e. ending with y_2, which is not affected by the buffer insertion.

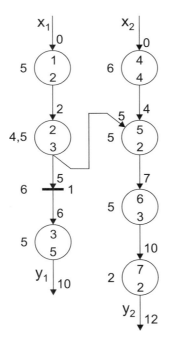

Figure 5 The modified EOG of Figure 3 by inserting a buffer for achieving $\min R = 7$

Based on the principle outlined above, a simple algorithm can be formulated for achieving a desired value of the restarting period R, if it is possible by inserting buffers. This algorithm is illustrated by the flow diagram in Figure 6 and is called SEPTUN, since it is derived from the separate tuning of the transfer sequences as shown above. It is assumed that the successor of actual e_i

is e_j, if any. Obviously, the minimal nunmber of inserted buffers is guaranteed in such a way.

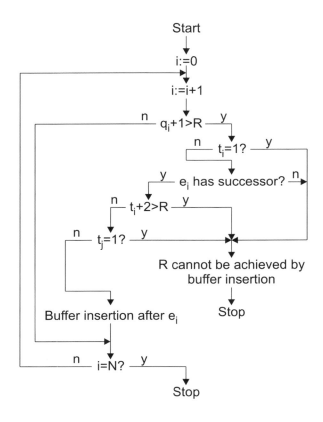

Figure 6 The flow chart of the algorithm SEPTUN (R denotes the desired restarting period, N is the number of operations in EOG)

3.2 Applying multiple copies of operations

To achieve a shorter restarting period than the value $\min R$ obtainable by buffer insertion, *multiple copies* of some operations must be applied. Let it be assumed that the desired restarting period for the transfer sequence in Figure 7(a) is $R = 8$. Applying the algorithm SEPTUN, the buffer insertion after e_3 can provide only $\min R = 22$ as shown in Figure 7(b). Note that the buffers after e_1, e_2 and e_4 reduce q_i, whenever $q_i + 1 > 8$, and $q_i + 1 \leq 8$

is achievable by the buffer insertion. The role of the buffer after e_3 will be explained later. It can be seen that the limitation of the further reduction is represented by e_3.

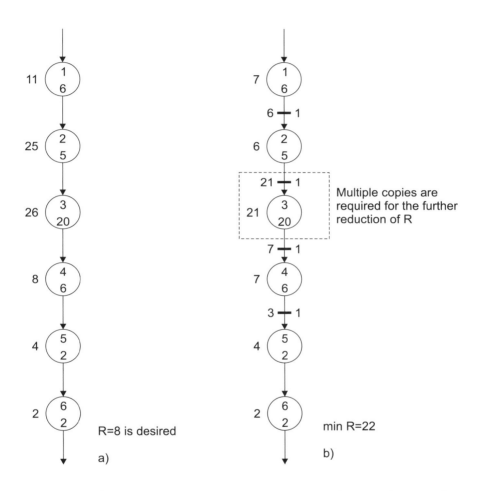

Figure 7 a) A transfer sequence with a desired value of $R = 8$. b) The buffer insertion after applying SEPTUN

Applying multiple copies of e_3 and the buffers on their input may allow the further reduction of the restarting period if a proper control is assumed (shown later). Let this situation be examined in Figure 8. If the control of the structure ensures that the input buffers of the copies are restarted with new data periodically after each other, then the arriving times of the first data can be expressed as follows:

$$v_{i_2,h} = v_{i_1,h} + R$$
$$v_{i_3,h} = v_{i_1,h} + 2 \cdot R$$
$$\dots$$
$$v_{i_{c_i},h} = v_{i_1,h} + (c_i - 1) \cdot R$$

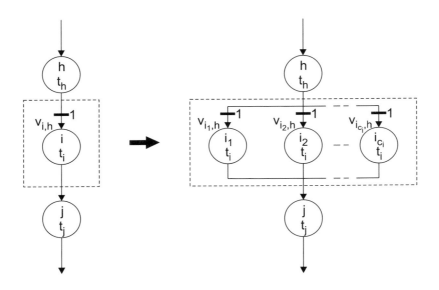

Figure 8 Replacing e_i by c_i copies

So, the first copy receives the first data at $v_{i_1,h}$ and its next data arrives at $v_{i_1,h} + c_i \cdot R$. Obviously, each copy has a time interval of $c_i \cdot R$ between its two subsequent data. According to the busy time condition (Assumption 2) for the input buffers of the copies

$$c_i \cdot R \geq 1 + t_i + 1$$

must hold. Thus, for a desired R, the minimal required value of c_i can be expressed as:

$$c_i = \left\lceil \frac{t_i + 2}{R} \right\rceil,$$

where the symbol $\lceil \ldots \rceil$ denotes the smallest integer which is greater than or equal to the value of the expression within these brackets.

Note that each copy of e_i needs an extra buffer at its input, since otherwise the reduced restarting period allowable only by applying multiple copies would hurt the busy time condition assumed for the elementary operations. Without these input buffers, new data would change the input of a previous copy too early. A proper control (shown later) is to be applied for enabling only the actual input buffer in each restarting period. Another control task is to properly enable the output data from the copies to the inputs of the successor operations. Note that the time interval between the arrivals of two subsequent data is exactly R at the common output of the copies.

Each data is stable for a time $c_i \cdot R - t_i$, since each start of a copy may change its output immediately (Assumption 3) i.e. by t_i earlier than the arrival of the next data from the next copy. If reordering and substituting the expression for c_i

$$t_j \leq c_i \cdot R - t_i \quad \text{i.e.} \quad \left\lceil \frac{t_i + t_j}{R} \right\rceil \leq \left\lceil \frac{t_i + 2}{R} \right\rceil$$

holds, then the interval of data stability is long enough for a proper execution of e_j. Otherwise, a buffer must be inserted at the common output in order to create $t_j = 1$, for which the above inequality always holds.

3.3 Combining the methods

If the algorithm SEPTUN inserts a buffer between e_i and e_j, then for further reduction of the restarting period at least

$$c_i = \left\lceil \frac{t_i + 2}{R} \right\rceil$$

copies of e_i are required to achieve a smaller desired value of R.

Considering again the transfer sequence in Figure 7, the desired value $R = 8$ requires at least

$$\left\lceil \frac{20 + 2}{8} \right\rceil = 3$$

copies of e_3.

In this case

$$t_4 > c_3 \cdot R - t_3 \quad \text{i.e.} \quad 6 > 3 \cdot 8 - 20$$

holds, therefore an additional buffer after the multiple e_3 cannot be avoided.

It may occur that a buffer inserted by SEPTUN is connected directly to multiple operations only. Obviously, such buffers can always be neglected, since the unavoidable input buffers of the multiple copies can take over their tasks.

Generally, it can be assumed that inserting buffers is not as expensive as applying multiple copies. Therefore, the reduction of the pipeline restarting period should be started by the SEPTUN algorithm and applying multiple copies is only the next step, if the desired value of R cannot be achieved by SEPTUN alone. In this case, the condition of optimum in realizing a desired value of the restarting period can be formulated, as to insert the minimal number of buffer registers and applying as few copies as possible. For this aim, SEPTUN can easily be interfaced to the calculation of number of copies, as shown in Figure 9 by the flow diagram of the algorithm called RESTART. It can be seen that preserving the buffers inserted by the SEPTUN algorithm, the minimal value of the busy time cannot be smaller than 2 in an EOG without a recursive loop (shown later), since an inserted buffer cannot represent a shorter busy time than 2. Thus, the shortest restarting period obtainable by the algorithm RESTART would be 3 without the last step before the stop label. This step, however, neglects the buffers inserted by SEPTUN, if each operation comes to be multiplied. This is always the case if $R = 1$ is desired in a loopless EOG, i.e. each operation is replaced by $c_i = \left\lceil \dfrac{t_i + 2}{1} \right\rceil$ copies.

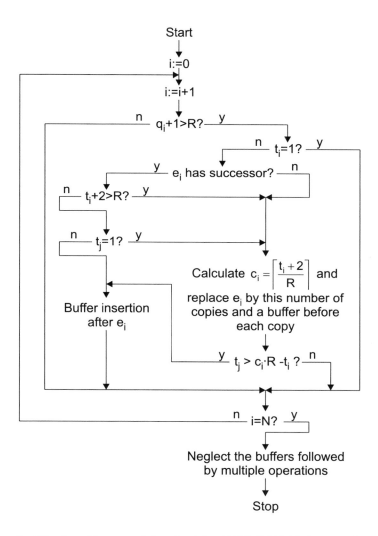

Figure 9 The flow diagram of the algorithm RESTART (R denotes the desired restarting period, N is the number of operations in EOG)

3.4   Symbolic representation of recursive loops

Recursive loops in an EOG require special handling, because the nature of a loop represents the lower limit in reducing the pipeline restarting period. In Figure 10, a symbolic loop representation is illustrated. It is trivial that the first operation of the loop can start to process new data only after the result obtained with previous data has already arrived from the last operation of the loop. Therefore, the duration of the loop is the sum of all durations inside it. In Figure 10:

$$T_i = t_k + t_l + t_m + t_n.$$

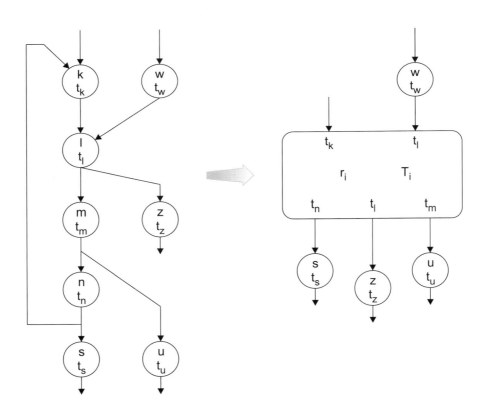

Figure 10   Symbolic representation of a recursive loop

Prescribing an extra clock cycle for the proper separation, the loop limits the restarting period to $T_i + 1$. In the case of more than one loop in an EOG

$$\min R \geq \max T_i + 1$$

holds. Following from the recursive character, the pipeline restarting period of the loop cannot be made shorter by inserting buffers between operations inside the loop or by multiplicating them. In fact, any extra buffers inside the loop would increase the total duration T_i. Therefore, the loop e_{r_i} must be considered symbolically as a single operation with duration T_i during the calculation of $\min R$. However, the algorithm RESTART has to calculate the busy times according to the loop operations representing the entering and leaving points of the loop in each transfer sequence involving the loop. Emphasizing this fact, a recursive loop is symbolized by a square in the EOG instead of a circle as shown in Figure 10. The whole loop is characterized by T_i and its inputs and outputs are labelled by the duration times of the entering and leaving operations affected by the transfer sequences involving the loop. Obviously, a recursive loop cannot consist of a single operation only, since a direct feedback from the output to the input of the same operation would hurt the constraint requiring stable input data during the whole duration time. This conflict can be eliminated in EOG by establishing the feedback of the single operation through a buffer register inserted at its output.

Many classes of the recursive calculations cannot be represented and handled so easily as shown above. The number of iterations, i.e. the depth of the recursion yielding a result at the loop output, may be greater than 1. This means that data circulates many times inside the loop until producing the result. Such types of recursive loops will be discussed later.

3.5 Handling of conditional branches (control and data domination)

Conditional branches in an EOG do not need special handling, since the condition checking can be considered as a special operation, the result of which enables the next operations receiving the conditions formally as normal additional data inputs. In this way, alternative sections are generated in the transfer sequences without any changes in the formal handling of the EOG except during the allocation procedure (shown later). In Figure 11, the symbolic representation of a simple conditional branch is illustrated. The condition checking is a comparator in this case and the alternative sections are closed by a multiplexer (MUX) operation, which is also controlled by the output of the condition checking operation. The same problem could be solved by other EOG structures as well. For example, if the condition checking output were connected only to the MUX operation, then the calculation would be also correct, but the two sections of operations would not be alternative any more. This is not advantageous during the allocation procedure (shown later), but executing both branches simultaneously with the condition checking may provide some gain in speed. The above simple formal handling of conditional branches requires operations with an additional third input transferring only Boolean values to control the MUX or to start branches. The role of the extra inputs is only the selection and they do not change the data processing after the selection. Therefore, the constraint of applying elementary operations with two inputs is not hurt, but the formal handling of the third input as an additional data input makes it possible to formulate the algorithm for synchronization of EOG without extra considerations to conditional branches (shown in the next chapter).

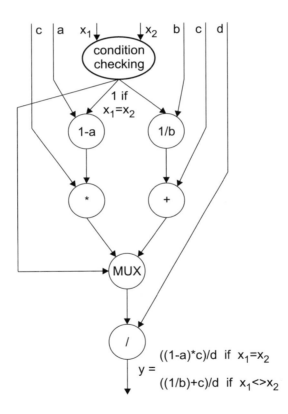

Figure 11   Symbolic representation of a conditional branch

If conditional branches are dominant in EOG and only few and simple elementary operations are contained by the branches, then the system is called *control dominated*. In such cases the function is driven mainly by external signals and the EOG can be considered as a graph representation of a finite state machine (FSM), which yields easily the structural description.

If conditional branches are not dominant, then system is called *data dominated*.

4

Synchronization

The dataflow-like character of the EOG implies that an operation can be started by the arrival of all of its input data. Another assumption for the operations is that they need all of their input data to be unchanged during the whole duration. This condition is not met automatically even for an initial EOG, and the modifying effects of the algorithm RESTART may also cause conflicts in this sense. The problem is illustrated in Figure 12. For the inputs of e_3, the data arrival times are $v_{3,2} = 2$ and $v_{3,4} = 11$, where the number 4 refers to the buffer as e_4 inserted between e_1 and e_3. If the pipeline restarting period $R = \min R = 12$, then the second data arrives at 23 and 14 respectively. This means that e_3 senses the next input change after $v_{3,4} = 11$ at 12, since the output of e_2 changes already at $v_{3,2} - t_2 = 14 - 2 = 12$. So, the first input data pair of e_3 is safely available only in the clock cycle 11, i.e. for one clock cycle instead of the required $t_3 = 5$ cycles. This synchronization problem may always arise if an operation has more than one input.

In Figure 13, let it be assumed that

$$b_i = \max(v_{i,h}, v_{i,r}, \dots) \quad \text{and} \quad b_i = v_{i,r}$$

In this case, b_i or $v_{i,r}$ can be called the earliest possible starting time of e_i.

For each $e_h \rightarrow e_i$, a time difference $z_{i,h} = b_i - v_{i,h}$ can be introduced. The second change of the output of e_h occurs at $v_{i,h} + R - t_h$. Therefore, the time interval, in which both input data of e_i are unchanged, is

$$v_{i,h} + R - t_h - b_i \quad \text{or substituting} \quad b_i = z_{i,h} + v_{i,h} :$$
$$R - z_{i,h} - t_h$$

Since the input data of e_i must be stable simultaneously for at least t_i, the inequality

$$R - z_{i,h} - t_h \geq t_i$$

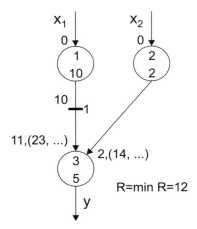

Figure 12   Illustration of the synchronization problem

must hold for the proper operation. If this is not the case, then an extra delay effect $p_{i,h}$ is required between e_h and e_i. The minimal value of this delay is

$$\min p_{i,h} = z_{i,h} + t_h + t_i - R.$$

The maximal allowable value of the delay effect is $\max p_{i,h} = z_{i,h}$, since a longer delay would increase the latency. Thus, the allowable interval for the delay effect is:

$$z_{i,h} + t_h + t_i - R \le p_{i,h} \le z_{i,h}.$$

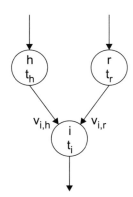

Figure 13   The general situation of the synchronization

If e_h is multiple, then the second change of the output of e_h occurs at

$$v_{i,h} + c_h \cdot R - t_h.$$

So, both inputs are stable in the interval

$$c_h \cdot R - z_{i,h} - t_h.$$

Therefore,

$$\min p_{i,h} = z_{i,h} + t_h + t_i - c_h \cdot R.$$

If e_i is a copy of a multiple operation, then

$$\min p_{i,h} = z_{i,h} + 1 + t_i - c_i \cdot R,$$

since e_h is always an input buffer register with $t_h = 1$ and only each c_i^{th} restarting period can cause changes at the input of an e_i copy.

The last expression must be applied if both e_i and e_h are multiple, since in this case the predecessors of the e_i copies are their input buffers instead of e_h.

Obviously, a negative or zero result for $\min p_{i,h}$ means that no synchronization problem arises on this input even without extra delay effects.

If the data path between e_h and e_i is inside a recursive loop and the other input of e_i from e_r is outside the loop and $b_i = v_{i,r}$, then let e_i be called a *loop-border operation*. In this case, the extra delay effect between e_h and e_i would increase the total duration of the loop. To avoid this drawback, the delay effect must be transferred to the input of the loop.

The first operation of a recursive loop, i.e. the input of the loop, is always free from the synchronizing problem, since the first feedback input data of this operation is an undefined initial value and so its arriving time can be considered as to be the same as the arriving time of the other input. Thus, the second and the further data cannot cause any conflicts because the restarting period is always longer than the duration of the loop. As an exception, special cases are presented in Chapter 9.

If the extra synchronizing delay effects were realized as delay operations with durations corresponding to the required values of the delay effects, then the restarting period calculated by RESTART might become invalid. Namely, the delay operations inserted additionally would produce new busy time sequences. A possible way of avoiding this problem is to realize the extra delays by connecting as many buffer registers after each other as the required value of the delay effect. Thus, the required number of buffers is $p_{i,h}$. In this way, the new busy time sequences cannot influence the restarting period calculated by the algorithm RESTART, since the duration of each new operation is 1. In this case, $t_h = 1$ must be replaced in $\min p_{i,h}$, because the immediate predecessor of e_i is always at least one buffer register, if the extra delay effect is required. Calculating $\min p_{i,h}$ with this assumption, a negative or zero result does not always mean now that the synchronization problem would not occur without extra delay effect, since at least one single buffer register has to be inserted as the immediate predecessor of e_i. Otherwise, $t_h = 1$ would not be allowed during the calculation of $\min p_{i,h}$ and the result with the original t_h value may be positive, indicating the synchronization problem.

In Figure 12, the interval for $p_{3,2}$ is as follows:

$$\max p_{3,2} = z_{3,2} = 9$$
$$\min p_{3,2} = z_{3,2} + 1 + t_3 - 12 = 9 + 1 + 5 - 12 = 3$$
$$9 \geq p_{3,2} \geq 3$$

A symbolic representation of the upper and lower bounds of the delay effect required for the synchronization is shown in Figure 14.

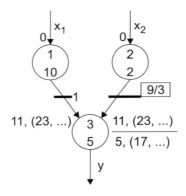

Figure 14   A symbolic representation of inserting buffers into the EOG in Figure 12

If e_i is a loop-border operation, then a single buffer register inserted as the immediate predecessor of e_i would increase the loop duration by 1, but it would allow $t_h = 1$ for the calculation of $\min p_{i,h}$. Thus, the minimal required number of buffer registers at the loop input is $\min p_{i,h} - 1$, the negative or zero value of which indicates that no buffer register is needed at the loop input, only the single one inside the loop. Generally, allowing a longer loop duration, a considerable reduction may be obtained in $\min p_{i,h}$ and so in the number of buffer registers at the loop input. Obviously, this solution can be applied only then, when the longer loop duration does not prevent achieving the desired restarting period for the whole EOG.

The algorithm SYNC based on the above considerations is summarized by the flow diagram in Figure 15. Besides the calculation of the intervals for $p_{i,h}$, the buffer representation of the required delay effects is also illustrated. The meaning of the ASAP and ALAP constraints will be discussed later in the chapter outlining the scheduling procedures. The algorithm can handle elementary operations having more than two inputs. The type of situations not involved by the flow diagram are shown in Figure 16, where more than one operation inside a common loop require synchronization. For example, it may happen that calculating separately the delay effects $p_{i,h}$ and $p_{m,j}$, even the inequality $\min p_{m,j} > z_{i,h}$ would hold. If the representing buffer registers were placed before the loop, then a new synchronization situation would occur for e_i. Namely, its input from e_h would be delayed to such an extent that its input from e_u would require synchronizing delay effects. Therefore, a repeated execution of the algorithm SYNC cannot be avoided to overcome this difficulty. After the first run, the new arriving times are to be calculated assuming the delay effect $\max(p_{i,h}, p_{m,j})$ at the loop input of such a structure. Starting with these new arriving times, the second run of SYNC always yields a correct synchronization.

It is trivial that the inputs arriving from different alternating conditional branches do not need any synchronization between each other, since they can never be active in the same restarting period. An example is the upper inputs of the MUX operation in Figure 11. However, there is a limitation for the execution time difference between the alternating branches. Namely, the proper execution along one of the alternating branches must not be disturbed by a possible execution along the other branch in the next restarting period. This means that a result produced by a branch started earlier must appear earlier and be stable for a proper time at the MUX output. In other words, the order in data processing must not be changed by alternation. Denoting the execution times of two alternating branches by T_{b1} and T_{b2} respectively and assuming $T_{b1} > T_{b2}$, the inequality

$$T_{b1} + q_{MUX} \leq T_{b2} + R$$

must hold, where q_{MUX} stands for the busy time of the multiplexer. MUX as an elementary operation must not be started while it is still busy with the previous alternation. For this reason, q_{MUX} cannot be neglected on the left side of the above inequality. Consequently, the upper limit of the time difference $T_{b1} - T_{b2}$ can be expressed as:

$$T_{b1} - T_{b2} \leq R - q_{MUX}.$$

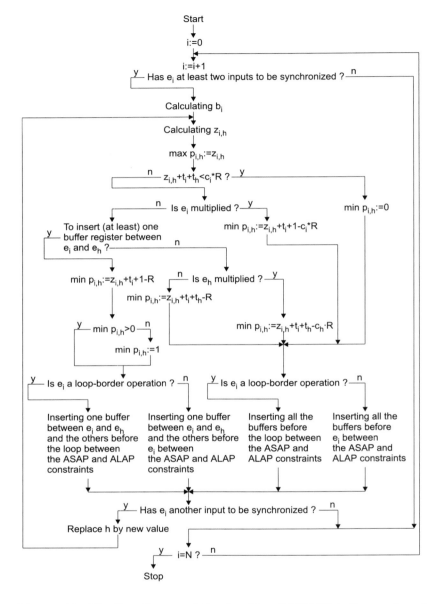

Figure 15   The flow diagram of the algorithm SYNC (N is the number of elementary operations in EOG)

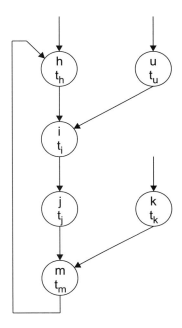

Figure 16 Illustration for the synchronization problem if several operations in a common loop need delay effects

If this inequality does not hold, then T_{b2} must be increased by an extra inserted delay effect (p_{b2}) having lower and upper bounds as follows:

$$T_{b1} - T_{b2} \geq p_{b2} \geq T_{b1} - T_{b2} - q_{MUX} - R.$$

Note that the upper bound is based on the assumption $T_{b1} > T_{b2}$ and excludes establishing the opposite situation, which would be beyond reason.

The above considerations for alternating branches do not refer to data synchronization, therefore calculating p_{b2} values is not a part of algorithm SYNC. However, the EOG (especially control dominated EOGs having many hierarchical alternating conditional branches) must be checked and branch delays p_{b2} must be inserted, if necessary. Obviously, this type of delay insertion has to be performed before executing algorithm SYNC, because p_{b2} values influence the data arriving times $(v_{i,h}, v_{i,r})$ in EOG parts after the affected alternating branches [VJL97].

The arguments for buffer representation of delay effects are valid also in this case.

5

Examples for applying the algorithms RESTART and SYNC

Example 1

The digital convolution algorithm is to be realized for three stages:

$$y_i = w_1 \cdot x_{i-2} + w_2 \cdot x_{i-1} + w_3 \cdot x_i,$$

where y_i denotes the actual output (result),
  w_1, w_2, w_3 are the constant weights,
  x_i denotes the actual input data,
  x_{i-1} and x_{i-2} stand for the input data received one and two restarts earlier, respectively.

The first step is to specify the elementary operations to be applied. Since inputs from the earlier restarts are to be preserved, two stage shift registers are convenient to use. Such a register can be considered as two consecutive buffers. Having stored data in the first of them, the shift into the second one is enabled only in the next restarting period.

Applying multipliers and adders as further elementary operations, the EOG is shown in Figure 17. The duration times are assumed as follows:

e_1, e_2, e_3	are multipliers with	$t_1 = t_2 = t_3 = 20$,
e_4, e_5	are adders with	$t_4 = t_5 = 10$,
e_6, e_7	are shift registers with	$t_6 = t_7 = 1$.

Since w_1, w_2 and w_3 are constants, each multiplier can be considered as having only one data input.

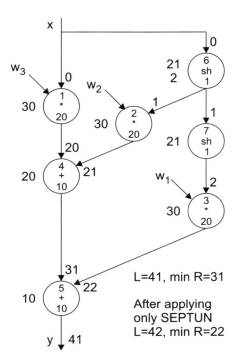

Figure 17   The EOG for the digital convolution algorithm

Following from the algorithm, the EOG can provide the first valid output only at the third start ($Restart_2$):

$$
\begin{array}{llllllll}
\text{Start} & (Restart_0): & w_3 \cdot x_1 & + & w_2 \cdot ? & + & w_1 \cdot ? & = & ? \\
& Restart_1: & w_3 \cdot x_2 & + & w_2 \cdot x_1 & + & w_1 \cdot ? & = & ? \\
& Restart_2: & w_3 \cdot x_3 & + & w_2 \cdot x_2 & + & w_1 \cdot x_1 & = & y_3 \\
& Restart_3: & w_3 \cdot x_4 & + & w_2 \cdot x_3 & + & w_1 \cdot x_2 & = & y_4 \\
\text{etc.}
\end{array}
$$

Without any modifications, the EOG allows min $R = 31$; after applying the algorithm SEPTUN, min $R = 22$ could be achieved. For the further reduction of the restarting period, the algorithm RESTART must be applied.

Let the desired restarting period be $R = 5$. The calculations according to RESTART are as follows.

No single buffer registers are to be inserted and for elementary operations e_1, e_2, e_3, e_4, e_5 multiple copies are required.

$$c_1 = c_2 = c_3 = \left\lceil \frac{20 + 2}{5} \right\rceil = 5$$

$$c_4 = c_5 = \left\lceil \frac{10 + 2}{5} \right\rceil = 3$$

The modified EOG is illustrated in Figure 18. The synchronizing delay effects are to be calculated only for e_4 and e_5:

$z_{4,1} = 1$
$1 \geq p_{4,1} \geq 1 + 1 + 10 - 3 \cdot 5 = -3$
$z_{5,3} = 10$
$10 \geq p_{5,3} \geq 10 + 1 + 10 - 3 \cdot 5 = 6$

It is trivial that the negative result for $\min p_{4,1}$ means that no synchronization problem can arise even without any delay effects on this input. Therefore, a negative value for $\min p_{i,h}$ is to be considered as zero in this case, since e_4 is a multiple operation and so the necessary input buffers represent $t_h = 1$ for each copy. Thus, the delay effects calculated for e_4 and e_5 can be symbolized in Figure 18 preceding the input buffers of the copies.

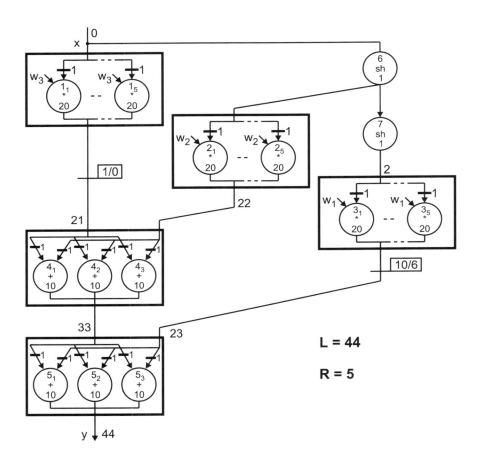

Figure 18   The modified EOG of Figure 16 after applying the algorithm
RESTART for $R = 5$

Example 2

The problem to be solved is to calculate the expression:

$$y_{i+1} = y_i + x_{1_i} \cdot x_{2_i} + \sqrt{x_{3_i} \cdot x_{4_i}},$$

where y_{i+1} is the actual output (result),

y_i is the output obtained at the previous restart,

x_{1_i}, x_{2_i}, x_{3_i}, x_{4_i} are the actual input data.

Applying adders, multipliers and SQRT operations as elementary operations, a possible EOG is shown in Figure 19. Let the duration times be assumed as follows:

e_1, e_2	are multipliers with	$t_1 = t_2 = 20$,
e_3	is the SQRT operation with	$t_3 = 20$,
e_4, e_5	are adders with	$t_4 = t_5 = 10$.

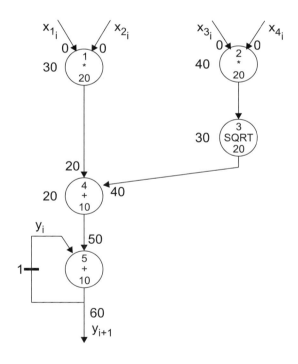

Figure 19   EOG for calculating the expression
$$y_{i+1} = y_i + x_{1_i} \cdot x_{2_i} + \sqrt{x_{3_i} \cdot x_{4_i}}$$

The buffer register at the output of e_5 is unavoidable, since otherwise e_5 would form the loop alone. Consequently, the direct feedback of y_i would be transient during the execution of e_5. This situation would hurt the assumption made for EOG.

Without any modifications, the EOG allows $\min R = 41$. Applying the algorithm RESTART only $\min R = 12$ can be achieved because of the recursive loop. The symbolic representation is shown in Figure 20. The calculations are as follows.

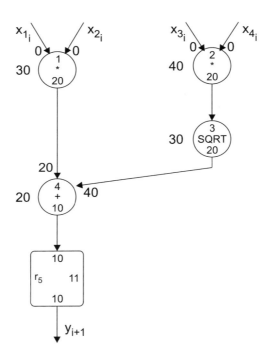

Figure 20   Symbolic representation of the recursive loop in Figure 19

A single buffer register is to be inserted after e_4 only and multiple copies are needed for e_1, e_2, e_3 to achieve $\min R = 12$.

$$c_1 = c_2 = c_3 = \left\lceil \frac{20 + 2}{12} \right\rceil = 2$$

Additional buffers cannot be avoided at the output of the multiple operations e_1 and e_3. The modified EOG is shown in Figure 21. The synchronizing delay effects are to be calculated only for e_4:

$$21 \geq p_{4,1} \geq 21 + 10 + 1 - 12 = 20.$$

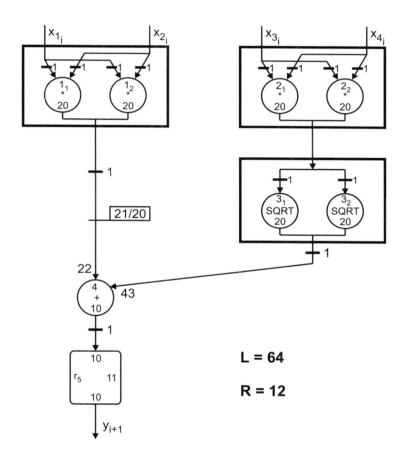

Figure 21   The modified EOG of Figure 20 after applying the algorithm
RESTART for $R = 12$

An alternative initial EOG for the problem to be solved is illustrated in Figure 22. In this case, the duration of the recursive loop is 20, therefore no shorter restarting period would be possible than $\min R = 21$. Obviously, this solution for the EOG is not advantageous. The general rule is that the duration of recursive loops should be kept as short as possible.

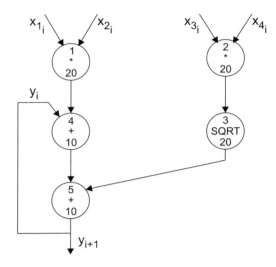

Figure 22   An alternative EOG for the problem in Figure 19

6

Scheduling as arrangement of synchronizing delay effects

The buffer representation of the synchronizing delay effects introduced in the previous chapters can be used advantageously during the scheduling procedures, because the buffers can be considered as delay units movable separately along certain parts of the data path without increasing the pipeline restarting period or affecting latency and synchronization. In this way, all possible situations can be simulated for the starting times of the operations, since the arrangement of the synchronizing buffers determines the starting time of an operation inside its allowed *mobility* domain. The data dependency in the EOG, the duration times of the elementary operations and the latency determine the allowed mobility domain for each operation. Two extreme cases can be defined as constraints for the mobility domain: each operation is started as soon as possible (ASAP schedule) or each operation is started as late as possible (ALAP schedule). For example, if all of the nine synchronizing buffers are assumed between e_3 and e_2 as shown in Figure 14, then this situation corresponds to the ASAP scheduling. Obviously, the synchronizing effect would not be changed, if all of the nine synchronizing buffer registers were placed at the input of e_2. This arrangement would represent the ALAP schedule for the EOG in Figure 12. Thus, the upper bound of $p_{3,2}$ can be used for calculating the maximal mobility of e_2. Considering the minimal required value of the synchronizing delay effect calculated as $\min p_{3,2} = 3$, the corresponding three buffer registers would not represent the same delay effect at the input of e_2 as they do between e_2 and e_3. The reason for this is that during the calculation of $\min p_{3,2}$, $t_h = 1$ has been assumed, which is not true any more if there is no buffer register between e_2 and e_3. In this case, $t_h = 2$ has to be taken into consideration because of $t_2 = 2$. Thus, the new value for $\min p_{i,h}$ transferred to the input of e_2 would be $9 + 2 + 5 - 12 = 4$. Another possible arrangement could be obtained if a single buffer register was left between e_2 and e_3. In this case two buffer registers, i.e. altogether three, would be enough at the input of e_2 for representing $\min p_{i,h}$, because $t_h = 1$ would be guaranteed by the single buffer register.

The algorithm SYNC always provides the ASAP schedule, if all the synchronizing delay effects $\max p_{i,h}$ are placed between e_i and e_h or (in the case of recursive loops) at the loop input. Starting from this schedule, the ALAP schedule can be obtained systematically by moving the delay effects step by step from the output of each elementary operation to its inputs. This procedure is to be started for the operations which produce the output data of the EOG and continued successively upwards until the inputs of the EOG are reached. During the relocation of the delay effects, the latency of the EOG must not increase and the synchronization obtained as the ASAP schedule must not be hurt. Two possible conflicts are shown in Figure 23.

If an elementary operation has more than one input *(collector property)*, then the delay effects originating from its output must be repeated at each input. Otherwise, the synchronization would be disturbed. If the output of an elementary operation is connected to the inputs of other operations *(distributor property)*, then different synchronizing delay effects may occur along each connection. In this case, only the smallest delay effect is allowed to be transferred to the inputs of the operation with the distributor property and this smallest value must be subtracted from each delay effect occurring along the other connections at the output. Obviously, the delay effects inserted into alternating conditional branches before executing SYNC are allowed to move inside the affected branch only. Otherwise, they would not properly decrease the execution time difference between the alternating branches. Based on these considerations, the ALAP schedule of the EOG in Figure 18 is shown in Figure 24, where only the values of $\max p_{i,h}$ are symbolized, since the delay effects according to $\min p_{i,h}$ would not mean the ALAP schedule.

Note that the delay effect 1 at the input of e_1 must not be pushed further to the input x of the EOG, because influencing e_6 is not allowed during the relocation of $\max p_{4,1} = 1$. In other words, the branching point at an input of the EOG is always to be handled as an elementary operation during the relocation procedure. Obviously, the delay effects at inputs w_i would only be formal, since these inputs are supplied with constant values which can be assumed to be available permanently.

Having the ASAP and ALAP schedules, the mobility time domain mob_i for an elementary operation e_i can be expressed as follows:

$$mob_i = l_i - s_i,$$

where l_i and s_i stand for the earliest possible starting time b_i of e_i according to the ALAP and ASAP schedule respectively.

To schedule an EOG means to assign a starting time for each e_i inside its mobility time domain mob_i, i.e. between its ASAP and ALAP constraints.

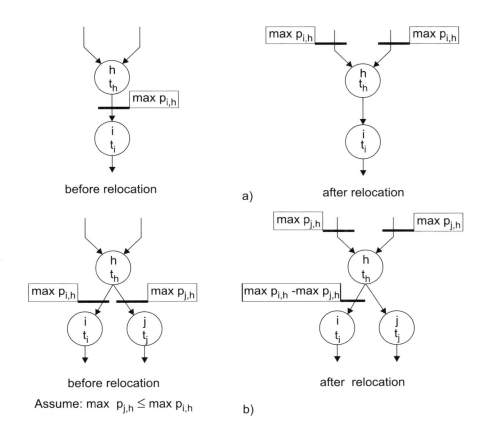

Figure 23   Relocation of synchronizing delay effects in the case of
operations a) with collector property, b) with distributor property

With the buffer register representation of the synchronizing delay effects,
the scheduling procedure can be formulated so as to arrange the buffer
registers of number $\max p_{i,h}$ inside the ASAP and ALAP constraints for each
e_i as has already been indicated in Figure 15. Each possible schedule could
be obtained if, starting with the ASAP schedule, the relocation procedure
towards the ALAP schedule was stopped at every possible intermediate step
for each individual buffer register of $\max p_{i,h}$ provided by the algorithm SYNC.
Even by relocating a single buffer register from the output to the input of an
e_i, a new schedule can be generated. Therefore, every possible arrangement
of the buffer registers representing the synchronizing delay effects $\max p_{i,h}$
establishes a different schedule for the EOG.

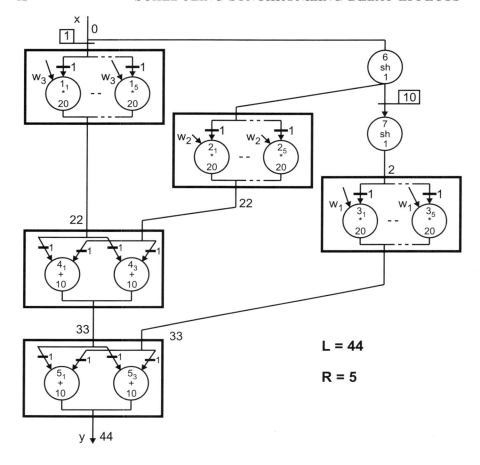

Figure 24   The ALAP schedule for the EOG in Figure 18

The buffer representation of synchronizing delay effects is beneficial for calculating the schedule as a buffer arrangement, but the number of buffers may be too large in practice. Therefore, the practical realizations of the above high-level synthesis results apply to other solutions for delay units, which are outside the scope of this book.

The aim of the scheduling in high-level synthesis is to ensure the best conditions possible for covering the elementary operations by real resources called *processing units* or *processors*. This is the *allocation* step of the synthesis and is detailed in the next chapter. However, it is trivial already at this stage that the schedule of the EOG has a strong influence on the efficiency of the allocation. For example, if the number and types of the processors are given in advance as constraints, then the allocation means to cover the elementary operations by their proper disjoint subsets, each of which is to be realized by a single processor. In this case, only such elementary operations can be drawn together in common subsets which are never busy at the same time, since otherwise timing conflicts would arise among the elementary operations sharing the same processor. Obviously, the quality of the solution and even the solvability of this allocation problem strongly depend on the schedule, since the concurrence of the elementary operations can be modified by choosing another schedule. How to determine the most advantageous schedule for the given allocation constraints is the problem to be solved by the scheduling methods. No algorithms exist for the optimal solution, since the problem is NP complete. However, many practical approaches to the scheduling problem have been proposed in the literature. The quality and performance of these methods can be judged only by comparing their results obtained for characteristic benchmark examples. The basic concepts of these practical approaches to the scheduling problem are detailed in a separate section after the most important constraints for the allocation have been introduced in the next chapter.

7

Allocation

The aim of the resource allocation algorithm is to decide which elementary operations are to be realized by common real processors [PP86, MR92]. It means that proper subsets of the elementary operations are to be found under several constraints (cost, area, data path complexity, processor type, etc.).

7.1 Covering non-concurrent operations

One of the possible strategies is based on the possibility that non-concurrent operations may share a common processor. It is trivial that the concurrence of elementary operations is strongly influenced by the length of the pipeline restarting period and scheduling. The four possible *time overlapping* (concurrence) situations between two operations are shown in Figure 25, where u_i, u_j and f_i, f_j denote the starting and finishing points of time of e_i and e_j, respectively and $b_j > b_i$ is assumed.

The finishing clock cycles can be expressed as $f_i = u_i + q_i$ and $f_j = u_j + q_j$. In a pipeline mode, the starting times of the operations e_i and e_j can be expressed as follows:

$$u_i = b_i + k_i \cdot R \quad \text{and} \quad u_j = b_j + k_j \cdot R,$$

where k_i and k_j are arbitrary non-negative integers representing the serial numbers of the data at the input of the EOG. It is convenient to distinguish k_i and k_j for e_i and e_j respectively, since their starts with data of different serial numbers may also cause concurrent operations. If e_i and/or e_j are multiple and their numbers of copies are c_i and c_j, then the expressions for the starting times of their $n_i{}^{\text{th}}$ and $n_j{}^{\text{th}}$ copies can be considered as generic forms involving also the above expressions in the case of $c_i = c_j = n_i = n_j = 1$:

$$u_{i,n_i} = b_i + (n_i - 1 + k_i \cdot c_i) \cdot R$$

and

$$u_{j,n_j} = b_j + (n_j - 1 + k_j \cdot c_j) \cdot R,$$

where $1 \leq n_i \leq c_i$ and $1 \leq n_j \leq c_j$.

Note that $n_i - 1 + k_i \cdot c_i$ and $n_j - 1 + k_j \cdot c_j$ represent the serial numbers of those data at the EOG input, which are transferred to be processed by the $n_i{}^{\text{th}}$ and $n_j{}^{\text{th}}$ copies of e_i and e_j respectively. The four overlapping situations can be characterized by the following inequalities:

$$u_i \leq u_j \leq f_i$$
$$u_j \leq u_i \leq f_j$$

Introducing the above generic expressions for the starting times,

$$\frac{b_i - b_j}{R} \leq K \leq \frac{b_i - b_j + q_i}{R}$$
$$\frac{b_i - b_j}{R} \geq K \geq \frac{b_i - b_j - q_j}{R}$$

can be obtained, where

$$K = n_j - n_i + k_j \cdot c_j - k_i \cdot c_i. \tag{7.1}$$

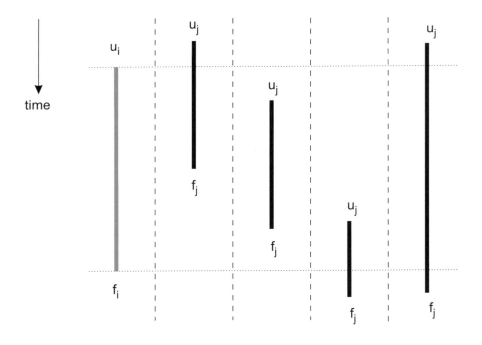

Figure 25   Concurrence situations of operations

The left sides of both inequalities are identical, therefore considering also the relations between the right sides, they can be substituted by a single inequality as the necessary and sufficient condition for the concurrence of e_i and e_j:

$$\frac{b_i - b_j - q_j}{R} \leq K \leq \frac{b_i - b_j + q_i}{R} \tag{7.2}$$

The operations e_i and e_j are overlapping in time, i.e. concurrent if and only if inequality (7.2) holds at least for one integer K satisfying equation (7.1). Based on this result, the necessary and sufficient condition can also be expressed for the non-concurrence of e_i and e_j. Firstly, let $c_i = c_j = n_i = n_j = 1$ be assumed, i.e. neither e_i nor e_j is multiple. In this case, any integer K satisfying inequality (7.2) excludes the non-concurrence. The non-existence of such integer K requires that the integer part of the left and the right sides of inequality (7.2) must be equal:

$$\frac{b_i - b_j - q_j}{R} = INT + FR1$$
$$\frac{b_i - b_j + q_i}{R} = INT + FR2,$$

where INT and $FR1$, $FR2$ denote the integer and the fraction parts respectively. (For example, the value -1.56 involves $INT = -1$ and $FR = -0.56$.)

The assumption $b_j > b_i$ implies that the left side of inequality (7.2) and so INT, $FR1$, $FR2$ are all negative. Expressing INT from the above first equality:

$$INT = \frac{b_i - b_j - q_j}{R} - FR1$$

and substituting it in the second one:

$$FR2 - FR1 = \frac{q_i + q_j}{R}$$

can be obtained. Since $FR2 > FR1$ and both are negative, $FR2 - FR1 < 1$ holds. Thus,

$$\frac{q_i + q_j}{R} < 1$$

or

$$q_i + q_j < R \tag{7.3}$$

can be written, as a trivial necessary condition for the non-concurrence. This expresses that the sum of the busy times of e_i and e_j must be shorter than the restarting period, otherwise the overlapping could not be avoided. Another necessary condition can be concluded from the requirement that the right side of inequality (7.2) must be negative:

$$\frac{b_i - b_j + q_i}{R} < 0$$

or, simplified,

$$b_j > b_i + q_i, \tag{7.4}$$

which is also trivial, since the time difference between the starting time of e_j should occur later than the end of busy time of e_i, if $b_j > b_i$. Otherwise, the non-concurrence would be hurt. However, inequality (7.4) alone is only a necessary condition of the non-concurrence, since for example, it holds also for the case $b_j = b_i + R$, which involves the concurrence of e_i and e_j in the second restarting period. Such situations can be excluded by considering that $FR2$ must not be zero for the non-concurrence, i.e. the right side of inequality (7.2) must not be equal to INT, otherwise INT would be the integer solution for K. Obviously, $FR1 = 0$ cannot occur, because $FR2 > FR1$ and both are negative.

Thus:

$$\frac{b_i - b_j + q_i}{R} < INT$$

and introducing the expression for the common integer part of both sides of inequality (7.2):

$$\frac{b_i - b_j + q_i}{R} < Int\left(\frac{b_i - b_j - q_j}{R}\right), \tag{7.5}$$

where $Int(\ \dots\ )$ denotes the integer part as defined for INT.

If all of the inequalities (7.3), (7.4) and (7.5) hold, then they represent together the necessary and sufficient condition for the non-concurrence in the case of $c_i = c_j = 1$, because these conditions are just sufficient for excluding the existence of an integer K solution in inequality (7.2).

If c_i or c_j or both of them differ from 1, i.e. e_i or e_j are multiple, then inequality (7.2) always has integer solutions for K, because the length IL of the interval for K is always greater than or equal to 1 in this case:

$$IL = \frac{q_i + q_j}{R} \geq 1,$$

since $q_i/R > 1$ or $q_j/R > 1$ holds, if e_i or e_j is multiple. Therefore, the non-concurrence would require that no integer solution of K satisfies equation

(7.1) for any non-negative integer values of k_i and k_j as variables. It can be proven that such values of k_i and k_j can be found for each integer solution of K. This means that e_i and e_j are always concurrent if at least one of them is multiple. For the proof, let inequality (7.2) be rearranged as follows:

$$\frac{b_i - b_j - q_j}{R} - n_j + n_i + k_i \cdot c_i \leq k_j \cdot c_j \leq \frac{b_i - b_j + q_i}{R} - n_j + n_i + k_i \cdot c_i$$

Choosing a positive integer k_i which makes both sides positive and introducing the notation:

$$A = \frac{b_i - b_j}{R} - n_j + n_i + k_i \cdot c_i,$$

inequality (7.2) can be expressed as

$$\frac{A - q_j}{R} \leq k_j \cdot c_j \leq \frac{A + q_i}{R}$$

Obviously, the length of the interval for $k_j \cdot c_j$ is the same as it has been for K before the rearrangement. Since $IL \geq k_i \cdot c_j$ holds, there exists at least one non-negative k_j which satisfies the above inequality, i.e. inequality (7.2). For the proof, this condition can be rewritten as follows:

$$k_j \cdot c_j \leq \frac{q_i + q_j}{R}$$

Let k_j be expressed as:

$$k_j \leq \frac{q_i + q_j}{R \cdot c_j}$$

If the right side of the above equality is always greater than 1, then the proof is completed:

$$\frac{q_i + q_j}{R \cdot c_j} > 1, \quad \text{or} \quad \frac{q_i + q_j}{R} > c_j$$

Let c_j be substituted by its expression derived from the calculation rule according to the algorithm RESTART:

$$\frac{q_i + q_j}{R} > \frac{t_j + 2}{R},$$

or

$$q_i + q_j > t_j + 2,$$

because

$$q_i \geq 2 \quad \text{and} \quad q_j > t_j.$$

At this stage, the proof is complete, since no constraints have been assumed for c_j and non-negative integer values for k_i and k_j can always be found in the above way.

Note that it was assumed for the proof that the minimal numbers of copies have been applied for the restarting period. Therefore, the copies of multiple operations are always concurrent if the minimal numbers of copies have been determined by the algorithm RESTART. In this case, it is obvious that the multiple copies of the same e_i overlap each other and their new restarts occur just after the end of their busy state (at most one clock cycle later because of taking the next greater integer for c_i). This means that there is not enough free time for a copy to be non-concurrent with any kind of elementary operations, since even the shortest busy time is two clock cycles.

Conditional branches in EOG need special consideration during the concurrence checking. If e_i and e_j are in separate alternating branches of the same conditional checking, then they never start to process the same EOG input data, i.e. $n_i - 1 + k_i \cdot c_i = n_j - 1 + k_j \cdot c_j$ never holds and so $K = 0$ cannot occur. Therefore, the solution $K = 0$ does not exclude the non-concurrence. Obviously, any nonzero integer solutions for K exclude the non-concurrence. In the case of $c_i = c_j = n_i = n_j = 1$, it means that the non-concurrence can hold only if the left side of the inequality (7.2) is greater than -1 and the right side of it is smaller than $+1$:

$$\frac{b_i - b_j - q_j}{R} > -1 \quad \text{and} \quad \frac{b_i - b_j + q_i}{R} < +1, \quad \text{or rewritten:}$$

$$b_j + q_j < b_i + R \tag{7.6}$$

$$b_i + q_i < b_j + R \tag{7.7}$$

The above inequalities together express the fact that for non-concurrence the busy time of one of the operations must be finished before the start of the other one in the next restarting period. These conditions involve the most pessimistic assumption that the conditional branches may be started alternately in each restarting period. If $c_i = c_j = n_i = n_j = 1$ and both of the inequalities (7.6) and (7.7) hold, then they represent the necessary and sufficient condition for non-concurrence in the case of operations in separate branches of the same conditional checking. Namely, these conditions represent the only possibility for excluding any nonzero integer K from the solutions of inequality (7.2). If either e_i or e_j is multiple, then for obtaining $K = 0$ as the only integer solution of inequality (7.2), the following upper bound for c_i and

c_j must not be exceeded. By adding both sides of inequalities (7.6) and (7.7),

$$\frac{q_i}{R} + \frac{q_j}{R} < 2$$

can be obtained, which can hold if at most only one of q_i/R and q_j/R is greater than 1. This means that at most one of c_i and c_j can be 2 and the other must be 1, i.e. $c_i + c_j \leq 3$, provided that c_i and c_j are determined by the algorithm RESTART. In consequence, the non-concurrence of multiple operations being in separate branches of the same conditional checking is possible only in the cases $c_i = 2$, $c_j = 1$ or $c_i = 1$, $c_j = 2$. This result can easily be explained as follows. If a multiple operation has only two copies, then the busy times of each copy do not last longer than the end of every second restarting period. Otherwise, the algorithm RESTART would not calculate two copies. Thus, each copy is free in a time interval of every second restarting period. This interval may allow the non-concurrence with a non-multiple operation from an alternative conditional branch, provided that inequalities (7.6) and (7.7) hold. This situation is sufficient for the non-concurrence even in the most pessimistic case (if the conditional branches are started alternately in each restarting period). Obviously, more copies would not allow non-concurrence, because their busy times would completely cover at least two restarting periods and so the pessimistic alternating turn of the conditional branches would exclude the non-concurrence.

The conditional branches may be hierarchically nested and interconnected. In these cases, the conditions according to inequalities (7.6) and (7.7) are applicable only if e_i and e_j are in such separate conditional branches which mutually exclude each other, i.e. never process the same EOG input data. Obviously, if this is not the case, then $K = 0$ can occur and so the non-concurrence conditions cannot be relaxed.

Based on the above considerations, the algorithm of the concurrence checking (CONCHECK) is summarized in the flow chart of Figure 26.

Obviously, multiple copies of the same elementary operation cannot be covered by a common processor based on the non-concurrence property. If, however, the processor library to be used contains so-called *structurally pipelined* processors, then this type of processor can cover several copies of a multiple elementary operation. Namely, *structural pipelining* means that the processor is able to accept new data before completing the previous one (see later in Chapter 11). A possible realization is the case in which an elementary operation is multiple and considered as a processor. Thus, multiplying the elementary operations is a possible case of forming structurally pipelined processors. Therefore, using such processors, the result obtained by the algorithm CONCHECK may be improved, since the copies of the same multiple elementary operations can be covered additionally by common

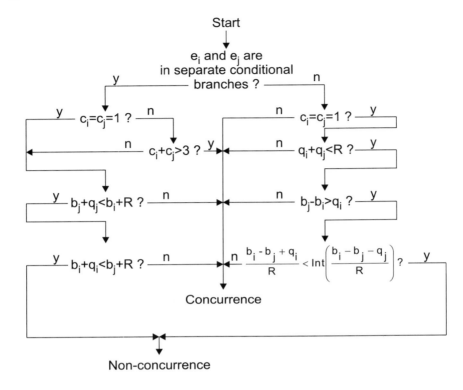

Figure 26   Flow diagram of the algorithm CONCHECK if $b_j > b_i$ is assumed

structurally pipelined processors.

It can be proven [AB96] that concurrence is a compatibility relation between two operations. Based on the above conditions, the compatibility checking can be executed for each pair of operations. The maximal compatibility or incompatibility classes can be obtained by the well-known algorithms [Lip91]. For finding the proper subsets of operations to be realized by common processors, a proper cover must be constructed with respect to the actual constraints for the processors.

7.2   Topological cover of operations

Another strategy of allocation could be the splitting of the EOG into parts containing data-connected operations. These parts specify the processors to be realized. The constraints for forming the processors may be the number and complexity of the operations to be combined in common processors or the simplicity of the data connections between the processors and in many cases the regularity of the structure. As an example for the regularity, let the EOG of the digital convolution algorithm in Figure 17 be considered. In Figure 27, this EOG is completed with the dotted adder and shift register. The synchronizing delay effects are to be calculated for e_4 and e_5 only. If the $\min p_{i,h}$ values are applied, then no extra buffers are required, since

$$\min p_{4,2} = \min p_{5,3} = 9 + 10 + 10 - 31 = -2.$$

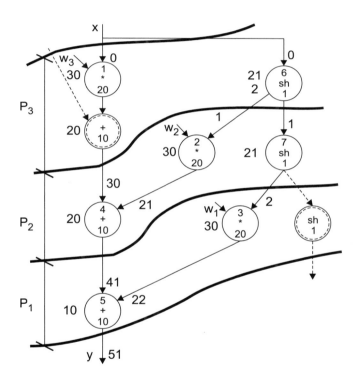

Figure 27 Completion and splitting of the EOG in Figure 17

It can be seen that the dotted additional elementary operations do not affect the restarting period, but make the EOG look symmetrical. Therefore, the separation of identical EOG parts becomes possible as indicated by the lines crossing the EOG. Each part may form an identical processor as shown in Figure 28 with the input-output specification as follows:

$$y_{out} = y_{in} + w_i \cdot x_{in}$$
$$x_{out} = x_{in-1},$$

where x_{in-1} denotes the input data that occurred one restart earlier than the actual one.

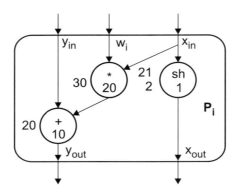

Figure 28   The internal structure of a processor obtained in Figure 27

The regular structure consisting of such processors is illustrated in Figure 29, which is similar to one of the systolic realizations of the digital convolution algorithm [Kun82].

Finding or establishing the symmetry of an EOG cannot be executed systematically without intuition and trial-and-error iterations. This task may become more difficult after the algorithms RESTART and scheduling, since the arrangements of extra delay effects and multiple copies of operations may eliminate even the inherent symmetry of the initial EOG. For example, the EOG in Figure 18 would be more difficult for establishing identical parts by completion outlined above and a completion usually needs a reschedule.

Having read Chapters 1 to 7, solving Problems 1 to 5 (Chapter 16) is advised.

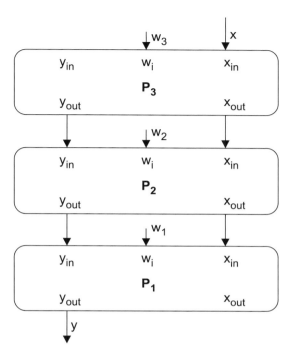

Figure 29   Systolic realization of the digital convolution algorithm

8

Combinatorial and asynchronous operations

So far, the shortest duration of an elementary operation has been assumed to be 1, i.e. one clock cycle. However, in many cases, some operations represent combinational and asynchronous functions (referred to as non-synchronous), the execution time of which is much shorter than a clock cycle or a non-integer multiple of the clock cycle [VJL97]. If such operations occur often in an EOG, it would be a loss in speed to wait until the end of the clock cycle each time before starting the next operation. To adjust the length of the clock cycle (i.e. the clock frequency) to the duration of these non-synchronous operations would not be a good solution. In this case, one clock cycle would be the duration of the fastest non-synchronous operation. As a consequence, the buffers could not be handled with duration of one clock cycle any more, since their operation needs one original clock cycle. If the duration of the buffers were considered longer than 1, then the effect of buffer insertion in algorithm RESTART would not be valid any more. The simple applicability of algorithm SYNC and CONCHECK would also be doubtful in this case.

A better solution is the pre-processing of EOG by assuming a fractional execution time for non-synchronous operations. The fractional duration time may be an arbitrary fraction or a multiple of the fastest synchronous operation, that is, of the buffer. The first step of the pre-processing is to detect transfer sequences of the following structure:

$$e_i \rightarrow \{Ne_z\}_{z=1}^m \rightarrow e_j,$$

where Ne_z denotes the non-synchronous operations, and the symbol $\{\dots\}$ represents an uninterrupted Ne_z sequence of an arbitrary length m.

Let $m = 1$ be assumed first, i.e. the transfer sequence contains only a single Ne_z (Figure 30).

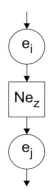

Figure 30   Transfer sequence with asynchronous elements

Ne_z cannot store data, therefore e_i must be considered to be busy

1. during its own execution time (t_i), and

2. during the execution time of Ne_z $(\underline{t}_z)$, and

3. during the execution time of e_j (t_j), since Ne_z is of combinatorial or asynchronous character.

Thus,

$$q_i = t_i + \underline{t}_z + t_j$$

If q_i limits the restarting period and t_i, t_j are both over one (clock cycle), then the most effective buffer insertion yields single buffers before and after Ne_z. This modification changes the influence of the non-synchronous transfer sequence on the restarting period. Now, the non-synchronous part starts after a buffer and ends with a buffer. The buffer before Ne_z has a busy time:

$$q_{p1} = 1 + \underline{t}_z + 1.$$

Consequently, a non-synchronous part of a transfer sequence represents a limitation to the restarting period:

$$\underline{t}_z + 3 \le R.$$

If $\underline{t}_z + 3 > R$ is required, then applying multiple copies of Ne_z would be necessary simply according to algorithm RESTART. Let the replication of Ne_z be neglected in further discussion. In other words, it is assumed that the EOG does not contain longer $\underline{t}_z$ than $R - 3$.

If $m = 1$ and

$$t_i + \underline{t}_z + t_j + 1 > R$$

holds, then a desired R can always be achieved with a lower limit $\underline{t}_z + 3$ by inserting a buffer before Ne_z and – if necessary – after it, too.

If

$$t_i + \underline{t}_z + t_j + 1 \leq R,$$

then there is no need for extra buffer insertion, and a virtual execution time $t_{v,i}$ of e_i can be introduced:

$$t_{v,i} = \lceil t_i + \underline{t}_z \rceil$$

Using this virtual duration also for an inserted buffer preceding Ne_z, the non-synchronous operation can be handled as non-existent during algorithm RESTART.

If $m > 1$, and

$$t_i + \sum_{z=1}^{m} \underline{t}_z + 1 \leq R$$

then the method is the same as shown above; the only difference is that $\underline{t}_z$ should be replaced by $\sum\limits_{z=1}^{m} \underline{t}_z$:

$$t_{v,i} = \left\lceil t_i + \sum_{z=1}^{m} \underline{t}_z \right\rceil$$

If, however,

$$t_i + \sum_{z=1}^{m} \underline{t}_z + t_j + 1 > R,$$

then the procedure is more complex. The goal is to divide the non-synchronous sequence into smaller sub-sequences by inserting buffers. If the first buffer is inserted after k non-synchronous operations ($k < m$), then

$$q_i = t_i + \sum_{z=1}^{k} \underline{t}_z + 1,$$

which represents a lower limit for the desired R:

$$\min R = t_i + \sum_{z=1}^{k} \underline{t}_z + 2.$$

To applying the least number of buffers possible, the non-synchronous subsequence between e_i and the first inserted buffer should be as long as possible. Consequently, the desired R sets an upper limit for $\sum_{z=1}^{k} t_z$:

$$\max \sum_{z=1}^{k} t_z = R - t_i - 2.$$

In other words, the first buffer must be placed inside the non-synchronous sequence at the end of this time interval after the start of the first Ne_z. The place of the next buffer (after the next n pieces of non-synchronous elements) can be determined similarly, but the direct predecessor of the next non-synchronous subsequence is a buffer now. Therefore, the interval must be calculated by replacing $t_i = 1$:

$$\max \sum_{z=k+1}^{n} t_z = R - 3.$$

This procedure should be continued until a proper approach to e_j is found. Let $\sum_{z=m-k+1}^{m} t_z$ denote the total execution time of h pieces of non-synchronous elements between the last inserted buffer and e_j. In this case

$$\sum_{z=m-k+1}^{m} t_z + t_j + 2 \leq R$$

must hold. Therefore, the maximal time distance allowed between the last buffer and e_j is

$$\max \sum_{z=m-k+1}^{m} t_z = R - t_j - 2.$$

If e_i is a replicated (multiple) operation, then the common output of the copies is assumed to be stable for $c_i \cdot R - t_i$ clock cycles. If

$$c_i \cdot R - t_i \geq \sum_{z=1}^{m} t_z + t_j,$$

then no buffer insertion is needed. If

$$c_i \cdot R - t_i < \sum_{z=1}^{m} t_z + t_j,$$

then the place of the first inserted buffer is to be calculated from the inequality

$$c_i \cdot R - t_i \geq \sum_{z=1}^{k} \underline{t}_z + 1,$$

which yields the maximal value of $\sum_{z=1}^{k} \underline{t}_z$:

$$\max \sum_{z=1}^{k} \underline{t}_z = c_i \cdot R - t_i - 1.$$

Having read Chapter 8, solving Problems 7 to 9 (Chapter 16) is advised.

9

Multiple-process recursive loops

Recursive loops are usually considered to be unavailable to overlapped (pipelined) execution during the scheduling phase of high-level synthesis. This is caused by the special nature of recursive execution: the next iteration of an iterative algorithm may not be restarted before the result of the previous iteration is available, i.e., T_i cycles after receiving previous data. T_i denotes the loop duration of loop i, defined as the execution time of the slowest execution path inside loop i:

$$T_i = \max_{\forall \text{ path } \in \text{ loop } i} \sum_{e_j \in path} t_j$$

A restart period under T_i cycles is impossible in an EOG containing recursive loops. Should the system be operated with a restart time such that $R < T_i$ for some i, subsequent data would enter loop i before ending the previous iteration. Therefore, recursive loops in the EOG represent a lower bound of restart time :

$$\min R = \max_{i:\forall \text{ loop}} T_i + 1$$

Assuming that any additional buffers after loop operations are placed at outputs that are read by non-loop operations (Figure 31), no additional increase of T is necessary to find R.

There are some notable exceptions, however, to the general case. In some problems, recursive solutions calculate values of identical functions for different processes. In this case, operations inside the loop (*core of the loop*, or simply *the loop*) may contain data from several sources simultaneously as long as there is no collision. This way, the loop may apparently process data with a higher throughput than the loop latency would permit. Just as pipelined and non-pipelined execution differ, a pipelined recursive loop appears to read and write data at a higher frequency than its latency would indicate.

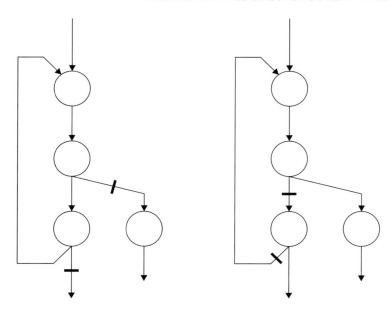

Figure 31   Placement of buffers after loop operations

Such an example is the centralized control of robots using the *computed torque technique*. Implementations of the computed torque technique require periodic calculations of a dynamic model for the robot joints to deal with changes in the environment. The calculations must be performed relatively infrequently, and the computational requirements are very high. It is therefore feasible to use a single implementation (i.e., single physical copy) for several different robots [Lan91].

9.1   Pipelined utilization of recursive loops

Decomposing a loop sequence to elementary operations makes it possible to tune the behaviour of the loop itself. Unlike in Chapter 5, recursive loops are not atomic operations during pipelined execution.

As time limits permit, it is possible to introduce new data (belonging to another process) to the start of the loop that runs through the loop without conflict with previous data. This overlapped execution exploits the inherent idle states of the loop (see Figure 32). With such a structure, more than one process may utilize the loop, if a strict schedule of data introduction is maintained. Such a loop is referred to as a *multiple-process (recursive) loop*.

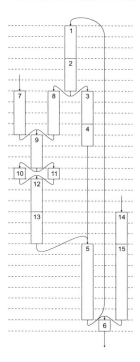

Figure 32   Execution times in a recursive data path

Processes forward data to the loop once in every $T_i + 1$ cycles and they fetch data at the same rate. The loop itself serves more processes and so takes and outputs data at a higher frequency than $\frac{1}{T_i+1}$. A *complete iteration* is equal to the time a process uses the loop, i.e., between the cycle of sending data to the loop for the first time and receiving data from the loop for the last time. An *iteration* (or *single iteration*) is the time of one turnaround of the loop, i.e., time of the longest execution path of the loop, plus any delay in the feedback branch. The number of iterations in a complete iteration is referred to as *loop depth*, g_i. See Figure 33.

Some recursive problems (such as some differential equation solvers) use their initial values only once. During iterative execution, each process works on the output of its previous iteration, ignoring any new initial data on non-feedback inputs. Recursive execution terminates, when exit criteria are met.

Another type of recursion is where both the feedback branch and the process supply data at every iteration. Such an example is exponential averaging on a given input sequence. This may be described as

$$y_i = y_{i-1} + a \cdot (x_i - y_{i-1})$$

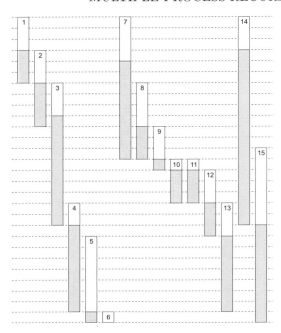

Figure 33   Operation busy times in the execution of Figure 32

It is obvious that an exponential averaging structure depends on both the previous result (y_{i-1}) and the current input (x_i). Therefore, a multiple-process loop must be properly synchronized so that

1. data exiting the loop and returning to the loop input must meet the next corresponding input data, and

2. no data overrun occurs inside the loop, i.e., data used and generated by any iteration does not get overwritten by data from the next iteration.

By using multiple-process recursive loops, separate processes may share the same resources in such a way that the loop is implemented only once. Every loop features a receptor as its first operation. The receptor handles feedback from the previous iteration and receives new data from the process. To tune the loop and to guarantee proper execution, the previous and the new data of the same process must be available at the receptor in the same cycle.

Process data creates a synchronization problem in the transfer sequences connected to the loop (*external synchronization*, page 71). Additional synchronization may be necessary inside the loop (see the next section, *loop scheduling*).

As the basic synchronization tool is the delay (buffer), a recursive structure optimized for pipelined execution is likely to execute slower than the non-pipelined loop. This speed loss may be small, especially for large loop latencies, as buffers cause a latency increase of 1 each.

9.2   Loop scheduling

The scheduling problem is illustrated by the easiest case, when the EOG consists of a single loop, therefore external synchronization is eliminated. In this structure $T = T_1$. It will be assumed that the graph contains only one receptor element at the beginning of the loop. The decision whether the data must stay in the loop for another iteration or the recursion has finished will also be made by this receptor element. This loop behaves similarly to a "test-before" construction, such as a `while` loop. To be able to schedule other types of loops, they must be transformed to "test-before" constructions. (For further information on loop transformations, see [ASU88].)

The loop is considered to be able to handle the data of M processes simultaneously. Iteration $M + 1$ features feedback from iteration 1. Data arriving at the first receptor will be the next fresh data of the first process. The first M initial values are passed to the loop with a period of R. (Generalization of these results to loops where there is a delay before the loop receptor is trivial. Except for a constant time offset, no additional modifications are required in subsequent formulas.)

To avoid a data synchronization problem between the feedback of the loop output (initial value of the next iteration) and new data, the loop duration (T) should be at least M times the restart time (R):

$$T = M \cdot R$$

As T is a function of given, fixed R and M values (set by the problem or hardware limits), the equation will hold just for special cases; otherwise, a synchronization problem exists inside the loop. To synchronize the loop, additional delay may be required. In this way the expression will be modified:

$$T' = T + p = M \cdot R + p$$

where p is the number of the inserted buffers (delay). The number of buffers is determined by the requirements of the restart time (p_s) and the feedback loop latency (p_f):

$$p = p_s + p_f$$

For the problem of scheduling, the loop for the aimed restarting time (calculation of p_s) any suitable scheduling method may be used to tune the opened loop. p_s is the sum of the number of the buffers inserted in the places where transfer scores and multiple operations make it necessary. This calculation takes place during RESTART.

Given p_s, the necessary additional delay, p_f may be expressed as

$$p_f = M \cdot R - T - p_s$$

where

$$T + p_s \leq M \cdot R$$

In a system where

$$T + p_s > M \cdot R$$

the feedback of the system will be slower than the system input (i.e., external data sources) and this must be taken into consideration when designing the external synchronization. In this case the feedback must not be further delayed, so $p_f = 0$ shall be used.

For further discussion, the necessary delay (p) is assumed to be zero. In this case, $T' = T$. Since changes in p affect every expression containing T, further results may be easily generalized to non-zero p. (No other changes than a time offset would be necessary in calculations.)

9.3   Classification of recursive problems

Data propagation properties may be classified as one of three main classes based on the number of iterations. Loop depth (g_i) is either a finite constant, a variable but finite value, or infinite.

9.3.1   Finite loop depth, variable number of iterations

Some problems iterate for a variable number of times before leaving the loop. These applications should finish within a finite number of iterations, otherwise they are unavailable for practical real-time usage. To prevent infinite iterations, the system should be equipped with a watchdog mechanism that finishes the iteration after a pre-set turn-around time, regardless of system state.

Iterative solutions of differential equations remain in an iterative state for a finite number of iterations, while the exact loop depth is data dependent; this kind of problem is a typical example of variable-depth calculations. For these calculations no exact time requirement rule may be given as the time needed to finish processing is unknown at design time.

Assuming the loop may process data from all sources simultaneously, process k may start its first iteration in cycle $(k-1) \cdot R$. Assuming the loop is of length $M \cdot R$, then

$$t_k = \underbrace{(k-1) \cdot R}_{\text{start}} + \underbrace{g_k \cdot M \cdot R}_{\text{iterate}}$$

if g_k iterations are required for one complete iteration of process k.

Obviously, the time needed for the *first* complete iteration to terminate (t_l) and new initial data to be introduced to the iteration is

$$\min_k t_l = \min_k R \cdot (g_k \cdot M + k - 1)$$

as data from process k enters the loop in time cycle $R \cdot (k-1)$ and it must run through g_k iterations, each using $R \cdot M$ cycles. A similar expression gives the termination of the last iteration:

$$\max_k t_l = \max_k R \cdot (g_k \cdot M + k - 1)$$

for similar reasons.

The above results may be extended to cases where the number of processes is much higher than the number that may be in the loop simultaneously. As shown below, the extensions are straightforward, but the result may be difficult to handle during the design phase. (This is the same problem as compile-time estimation of runtime behaviour in a data-driven environment.)

9.3.2 *Finite loop depth, constant number of iterations*

The method of treating special recursive loops may be applied to some applications that are not recursive. Such loops include `for` loops of high-level programming languages. For our purposes, these loop types may be treated as special recursive tasks. If the problem description permits, one may estimate the performance of such loops using the method outlined above.

In the case of, for example, a fixed-order FIR filter, the number of iterations is related to the order of the filter, which is constant for a given structure. To model this set of problems, we assume that the hardware has to put x initial values through the recursive calculations, i.e., x separate processes supply initial values. Every complete iteration of these values iterates in the loop for $g = g_0$ iterations. Non-overlapping execution would finish with these data in $g \cdot T \cdot x$ cycles: each iteration lasts T cycles, g of which are contained in each complete iteration (totalling $g \cdot T$ cycles), and x of these amounting to $g \cdot T \cdot x$ cycles.

Assuming there is no delay before the loop receptor, data from process k ($k \leq M$) enters the loop in cycle $(k-1) \cdot R$ (if process numbers start at one, as seen earlier). Each complete iteration requires $g \cdot T = g \cdot M \cdot R$ cycles, therefore, data from process k leaves the loop finally in cycle $(k-1) \cdot R + g \cdot M \cdot R$. The loop has no idle capacity before the data from process 1 leaves it. In cycle $g \cdot M \cdot R$, process $M + 1$ may provide input to the loop, since the complete iteration of process M ends, and process 1 does not introduce any more data. Similarly, process $\alpha \cdot M + 1$ may provide input to the loop in cycle $\alpha \cdot g \cdot M \cdot R$. Since the loop reads input from M processes before filling up with data, processes send data to the loop in groups of M (i.e., for suitable integer α, processes $\alpha \cdot M + 1$ and $(\alpha + 1) \cdot M$ may be active at the same time). With x processes, the last such group may be found as

$$(\alpha + 1) \cdot M \leq x$$

which, in turn, implies

$$\alpha = \left\lfloor \frac{x}{M} - 1 \right\rfloor$$

As x is a large number, we may assume it to be an integer multiple of M. (Otherwise, the number of input values may be padded to the nearest integer multiple of M, which does not affect calculations significantly if $M \geq x$, as shown later.) Since no idle time is desired, process execution starts immediately if the loop becomes available for its data. After starting execution for the first M processes, the loop may not take data from any process except those already using the loop (since the loop is fully utilized). In this case, as $\left\lfloor \frac{x}{M} \right\rfloor = \frac{x}{M}$,

$$\alpha = \left\lfloor \frac{x}{M} - 1 \right\rfloor = \frac{x}{M} - 1$$

The last group of M processes to utilize the loop therefore consists of processes $\alpha \cdot M + 1, \alpha \cdot M + 2, \ldots \alpha \cdot M + (M - 1)$, or, equivalently, $x - M, x - M + 1, \ldots x - 1$ The last of these processes, process $x - 1$, starts its complete iteration in cycle

$$\alpha \cdot g \cdot M \cdot R + g \cdot M \cdot R + (M - 1) \cdot R = R \cdot x \cdot g + (M - 1) \cdot R$$

Using a system with a complete iteration of T cycles on x different data requires $x \cdot g \cdot T$ cycles without overlapping execution. This result may be compared to the overlapped time, which is less than the non-overlapped requirement:

$$R \cdot x \cdot g + (M - 1) \cdot R \leq x \cdot g \cdot T = x \cdot g \cdot M \cdot R$$

as

$$M - 1 < M \leq x \cdot g \cdot M$$

Since x is large, i.e., $1 \leq x \cdot g$, the inequality holds. The ratio of hardware costs is

$$\frac{x \cdot g \cdot M}{x \cdot g + (M - 1)}$$

with a higher value indicating less idle time.

9.3.3 Infinite loop depth

Infinite loop depth is presented in the case of continuous calculations. Robots, for example, need to calibrate the dynamic model of their environment periodically [Lan91]. In this case the overlapped loop execution is usually slower than the non-pipelined version as modifying the loop for overlapping increases T (it inserts buffers to the data path). Note that the loop itself becomes slower during scheduling, but this leads to an increase in throughput as more data is processed simultaneously.

Substituting $g \to \infty$ into the above inequality shows the asymptotic gain in hardware utilization to be

$$\lim_{g \to \infty} \frac{x \cdot g \cdot M \cdot R}{R \cdot x \cdot g + (M - 1) \cdot R} = M$$

In other words, assuming infinite loop depth, M processes may still utilize a single loop, if proper overlapping is guaranteed. Of course, this requires loop scheduling and additional steps.

9.4   External synchronization

External synchronization will be illustrated on an example (Figure 34), which is a part of a data filter in voice transfer. The EOG checks the predictability (and compressibility) of voice transfer. Such a circuit may monitor digital audio transmissions and regulate sampling time.

The system is a model of the following:

1. Branch 7-8-9-10-11-12-13 is responsible for the adaptive tuning of the sampling time. This choice is based on the difference in signal energy: e_7 (SQR) produces the square of the signal value x_k, while e_8 takes another signal value and squares it. The difference of these signals is compared to a maximum (operation e_{10}) and a minimum (e_{11}).

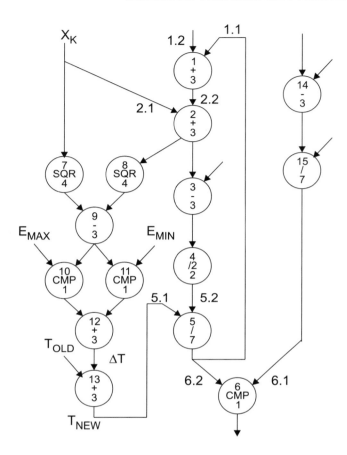

Figure 34   Data path of a system that monitors compressed
voice transmission

Should the difference exceed a given value, e_{10} outputs a negative value
as ΔT; e_{11} outputs a positive ΔT if the difference is close to zero. These
two factors are added to find the final change in sampling time in e_{12}.
Sampling time is therefore increased for a signal that does not change
in a long time. Conversely, sampling frequency is decreased if a signal
contains high-frequency components. The output of e_{12} is added to the
previous sampling time in e_{13} to update the value.

2. Branch 1-2-3-4-5 approximates the signal based on its previous
   behaviour. This model approximates the current value as if it were

following the average of previous samples. (It follows signal behaviour based on a digital low-pass filter, comparing the result to the actual observations (e_{14}, e_{15})).

3. Branch 14-15 measures the real signal. Its output is the slope of the signal, which is compared to the slope of the approximation in e_6.

This recursive algorithm contains all possible data conflicts. Synchronization problems are negotiated here in time order, which eliminates any iterative steps during the scheduling process. In this example two different, but not independent loops exist (the first follows the 1-2-7/8-9-10/11-12-13-5 path and the second one the 1-2-3-4-5 sequence). In the first step the second loop must be tuned to the critical recursive path, inserting extra buffers into the shorter path. As seen in Figure 35, nine delay cycles must be provided between e_4 and e_5. Similarly, an appropriate delay must be provided to synchronize measured values before connecting them to e_2, e_7, and e_{14}.

Even if the loop latency is 27 cycles, the loop may be operated with $R = 14$. As shown in Figure 36, if there is a two-fold overlapping of the loop during execution (i.e., $M = 2$), data from processes 1 and 2 (light and dark in Figure 36, respectively) do not affect each other.

Having read this chapter, solving Problem 10 (Chapter 16) is advised.

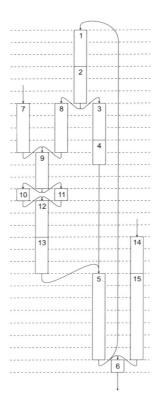

Figure 35   Execution timing of the graph in Figure 34

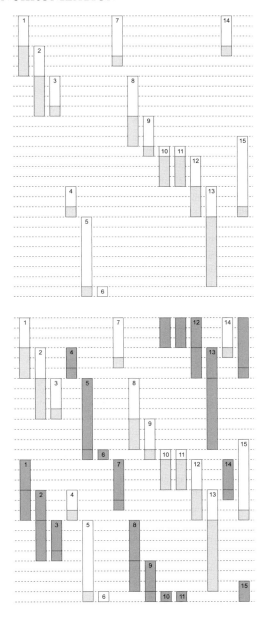

Figure 36 Busy times in non-pipelined and pipelined execution

10

Control principles

The scheduled and allocated EOG represents the structural design of the data path only. A proper control is required additionally to co-ordinate the elementary operations according to the EOG. This control has to ensure the correct data dependence and timing not only between the processors, but also inside the processors between the elementary operations covered by a common processor. Data multiplexing and demultiplexing are also to be controlled for establishing the required data connections between the processors covering more than one elementary operation. It is also a control task to synchronize the starting times and to distribute the input data for the copies of multiple operations. The control models are classified basically as *centralized* and *distributed control path*.

The aim of this chapter is only to illustrate the main classes of control structures. The practical solutions raise many design problems not mentioned here.

10.1 Centralized control path

Let the EOG in Figure 37 be considered as an example. Without detailing the scheduling and allocation steps (the duration times are not shown), let the processors $P_1 \ldots P_6$ be assumed as a result for the cover of the elementary operations as follows:

$$P_1 : e_1, e_5, e_{10} \quad P_2 : e_2, e_7 \quad P_3 : e_3, e_9 \quad P_4 : e_4 \quad P_5 : e_6 \quad P_6 : e_8$$

In Figure 37, the internal structures of processors are illustrated only symbolically. The elementary operations covered by a common processor are dotted, because they generally cannot be separated any more in practical realizations of the processor shared by them. Only due to this symbolic separation is it allowable to neglect the data multiplexing and demultiplexing inside the processors. Obviously, the buffer registers and the delay effects generated by the algorithms RESTART and SYNC need also proper control

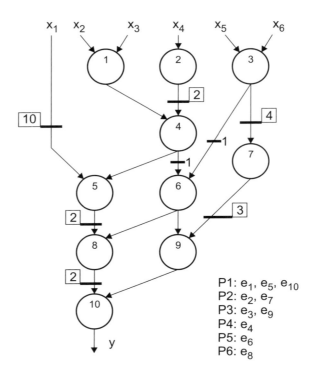

Figure 37 Example for covering the EOG by processors

signals in order to satisfy their timing constraints. The *centralized control path* is basically a *counter* driven by the system clock. The actual content of the counter determines the elementary operations and buffers to be started by producing the proper start signals ($st_1 \ldots st_{18}$). These output signals of the control path must be generated by a modulo R counter and decoder. In non-pipelined mode, each EOG component has a single start signal, since it is started at most once during the time corresponding to L, since each e_i receives a starting pulse (st_i) in every b_i^{th} clock cycle. In a pipeline mode, however, an elementary operation is started more than once during L depending on the value of L/R.

Note that the serial numbering of the start outputs in Figure 38 does not always reflect the order of magnitude of the counter content. For example:

$$(st_{11}) < (st_{10}),$$

where the brackets stand for counter content generating the given start signal.

It is trivial that e_9 must be started by st_{10} later than e_3 by st_{11} according to the data dependence prescribed by the EOG. Another remark to Figure 38 is that

$$(st_1) = (st_6) = (st_{11})$$

is to be assumed, i.e. e_1, e_2, e_3 can be started by a common signal. These operations receive data directly from the EOG input and so they start simultaneously, no matter how long the duration times are.

In a control-dominated system, the centralized control path is a finite state machine rather than a counter. In such cases, synchronous sequential circuits are the practical solutions.

As has already been shown in Section 3.2, multiple elementary operations need special control considerations. In Figure 39, the *internal control path* is based on a modulo $2 \cdot c_i$ counter and the $st_{i_1} \ldots st_{i_{2 \cdot c_i}}$ outputs must be generated in *1-from-n (one-hot)* code in this case. The input st_i receives a pulse from the main control path each time, when the start of the multiple e_i is required. Therefore, each st_i pulse must generate exactly two subsequent start pulses at the outputs $st_{i_1} \ldots st_{i_{2 \cdot c_i}}$, the first one for the input buffer and the second one for the copy being just in turn. This is the task of the *count control unit* in Figure 39. (The unavoidable output multiplexing and its control are not illustrated in the figure.)

The main advantage of the centralized control structure is its simplicity of implementation. Nevertheless, the centralized control has a disadvantage. Because of the concentrated placement of the counter, many control lines of different lengths should be connected to different points of the system. Therefore, the different delay effects and the large number of line crossings may cause difficulties in FPGA and VLSI realizations. To avoid this problem, the *distributed control structure* should be used.

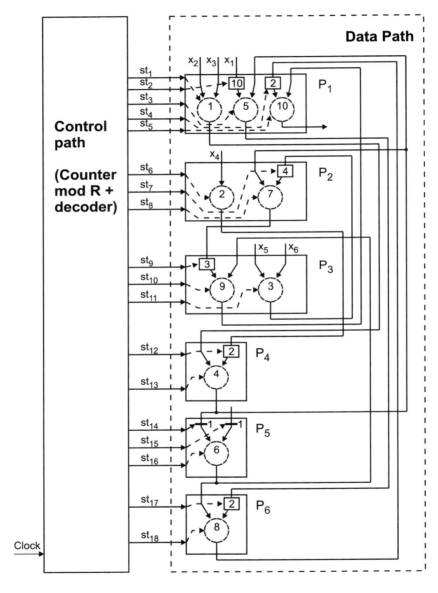

Figure 38   Centralized control structure for the EOG in Figure 37

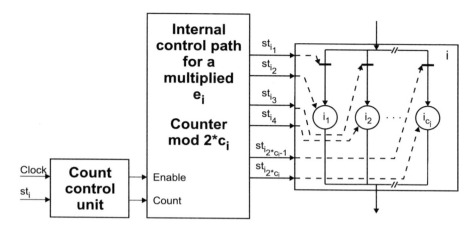

Figure 39   Control structure for multiple operations

10.2   Distributed control path

Distributing the control task among the elementary operations can eliminate the centralized control path. The dataflow-like character of the EOG and the constraints for the operations (see Chapter 2) require that the start signal (st_i) of an e_i must be generated only when every e_j, for which $e_j \rightarrow e_i$, has already finished the operation. Thus, each elementary operation must take part in generating the start signal of its next successors determined by the data connections (edges) in the EOG. For this aim, the busy time intervals of the operations (see Chapter 7) can be represented by signals on extra 1-bit connection lines chained through the EOG and accompanying each data connection. Such an extra edge as *busy line* can specify the busy state of e_i by the Boolean signal value B_i, as follows:

$$B_i = 1 \quad \text{if and only if } e_i \text{ is busy, i.e.} \quad u_i \leq t \leq f_i,$$

where t is the time parameter, otherwise

$$B_i = 0.$$

To evaluate the busy signals from the direct predecessors and to generate its own start and busy signal, these are extra tasks for e_i in the case of distributed control. Therefore, each e_i is supposed to be provided with an extra *distributed control cell (DCC)* as shown in Figure 40. The required function of a DCC_i is to generate the start pulse st_i in the same timing as the centralized control path does. This means that the system clock must be taken into consideration as time base, consequently DCC_i can be specified as a synchronous sequential machine. The specifications of all DCCs are identical except the duration of $B_{out} = 1$ which is determined by the duration (execution) time of the operation. With the input-output notations in Figure 41, the task of a DCC can be formulated as follows.

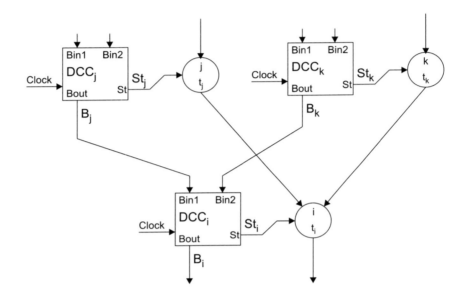

Figure 40   Completion of the EOG with distributed control cells

The cell waits for the falling edges on B_{in_1} and B_{in_2}. Having received both of them, the later one enables the next single clock pulse to the st output as st_i. The falling edge of this single clock pulse activates $B_{out} = 1$ as B_i which lasts exactly for t_i clock cycles. After the falling edge on B_{out}, the cell is waiting for new falling edges on B_{in_1} and B_{in_2}.

Such a simple sequential machine is to be realized for each elementary operation for performing the distributed control, yielding a *mixed data and control path*.

After the allocation step, the processors may represent many elementary operations also with the corresponding DCCs. Obviously, the DCCs inside the same processor can be realized only by a single sequential machine, but the multiplexing and demultiplexing of its inputs and outputs and the different $B_{out} = 1$ durations must be ensured.

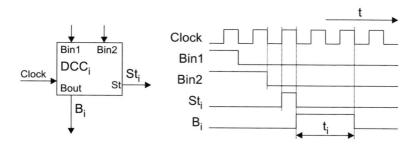

Figure 41   Specification of the distributed control cell DCC_i as a synchronous
sequential machine

If e_i receives the input data of the system in non-pipeline mode, then the
inputs B_{in_1} and B_{in_2} of DCC_i are to be connected to the output B_{out} of the
DCC belonging to one of the elementary operations, which produces the result
data at the end of the longest transfer sequence. In this way, e_i can receive
new input data only after a time corresponding to the latency. In pipeline
mode, the inputs B_{in_1} and B_{in_2} of DCC_i must be generated from outside as
often as e_i is to be restarted with new system input data.

The above DCC principle could be applied for realizing the distributed
internal control of multiple operations. Nevertheless, no simpler solutions can
be obtained in practice than the counter-based control path in Figure 39, since
the practical values of c_i need relatively short counters.

11

Scheduling methods

During the course of high-level synthesis the steps directly following EOG generation are scheduling and allocation. These steps are performed on a data-flow graph, a graphical representation of data dependencies in the system. In this EOG, nodes are elementary operations, with the directed branches between them indicating immediate data dependencies.

As data propagates sequentially through the data path, elementary operations are left idle until the arrival of the next data. The number of these inherent idle cycles may be decreased using *pipelined execution*. The overlapped (pipeline) method of feeding data to a system is the case where restart time is less than latency. It is possible to use pipelined execution in systems where the idle times of processors enable overlapping. If busy times do not conflict with each other, subsequent input values do not disrupt previous output before they are read from the outputs of operations.

The lowest "safe" restart time may be found using the execution time of neighbouring operations as shown in Chapter 3. As pipelined execution decreases overall idle time, data throughput is increased. There are two different methods of increasing utilization through pipelining. Structural and functional pipeline are two expressions often encountered in scheduling, even if their meaning is not always made clear.

Structural pipeline presents a method of speeding up execution inside operations. In this model, operations are implemented with internal overlapping, so that they execute multiple, consecutive stages. Each operation becomes available to receive data as its first stage finishes processing. As shown in Chapter 10, the busy time of the first stage is related to its execution time and that of its immediate successor (very similar to the relationship of q_i and t_i).

In structurally pipelined operations with more than three stages, the possible data introduction period is less than the actual time needed to complete all the calculations. Structural pipeline requires distributed control structures, more complicated than those of non-pipelined systems. (Control information and control flow of structurally pipelined operations may be synthesized as described in Chapter 10.)

In *functionally pipelined systems* the data path itself is used in a pipelined way. In such systems, operations execute without internal overlapping, i.e., they process inputs in an uninterruptible, single stage. As the operations themselves do not support pipelining, the graph itself serves as a source of overlapping operation. The control structure of functionally pipelined systems is very similar to the control of non-pipelined systems.

Since structural pipelining is based on complicated operations (i.e., they may not be called elementary), the method is outside the scope of our investigations. Control of structurally pipelined systems is a hierarchical, complicated process, and requires several additional steps beyond controlling a non-pipelined system.

Operation replication (as presented in Chapter 3) is similar to structural pipelining, but replicated operations are still elementary. The only control difference between elementary operations and replicated operations is additional control structures, which do not affect the internals of replicated operations.

Most of the available scheduling algorithms assume that elementary operations are able to process data t_i cycles after reading the previous value. Even if the actual duration is t_i, there are additional time requirements not represented in this model. As shown in Chapter 3, scheduling should represent the busy time of operations to properly model delay. Unfortunately, some of the available scheduling heuristics may not be easily extended to use q_i instead of t_i.

11.1   Stages of scheduling and allocation

An EOG before scheduling is a functional description where only the behaviour of the elementary operations is fixed. Given the implementation details, other parameters, such as timing and cost, may be found.

The scheduling problem attempts to find timings of elementary operations (a *schedule*) in such a way that the corresponding hardware realization is efficient. Scheduling is followed by allocation, where elementary operations are mapped to processors.

Allocation assigns the actual processor copy that will execute the operation; this is an instance of the graph colouring problem. The allocation graph of elementary operations has an edge between two operations if and only if their busy times overlap. The graph must be coloured in such a way that no operations of the same colour are connected by a branch.

The feasibility of a schedule may be checked immediately after scheduling or during allocation. A schedule is feasible if it may be built without violating one or more constraints set by the operating environment or manufacturing process.

As scheduling uses information based on some of the knowledge of the allocation method, certain allocation steps may be performed before scheduling. Such preliminary allocation-related steps may be described as "initial allocation". External constraints are to be taken into account during this stage. The usual types of constraints are latency (L), restart time (R), and hardware cost.

Latency must be kept under a limit in systems with a strict upper bound on delay between reading and writing system ports. Digital controllers used in process control are typically constrained by system latency. Controller latency is a lower limit of control loop *dead-time*, which has a serious impact on the control algorithm. In these applications, system latency is either an absolute limit ("hard real-time"), or a constraint which may be violated, but at an extremely prohibitive cost ("soft real-time").

As an increase of latency presents additional problems in the design of process control, it must not be increased over a feasible value (keeping latency under a constraint is a prerequisite of real-time operation). It is possible, however, to design for a given latency and find that a solution does not use all the available latency (Figure 42). As the scheduling plan sets the last operation e_4 to cycle 6, its output must be delayed one cycle in order to guarantee a latency of 7, should the system be prescribed to work with a latency value being equal to 7.

Restart time is critical in applications where data *must* be passed to the system with a given frequency. For data acquisition (*sampling*) applications, operating frequency is usually more important than latency. In such systems, reducing restart time is a gain worth the increase in latency. Decreasing restart time usually increases latency, as it may involve inserting delay to the data path.

Hardware limits are encountered in the design of systems where the realized hardware is bounded in some way, be it power dissipation, silicon area, or cost. Embedded systems, such as applications used in extreme environments such as outer space, for example, are typically constrained by all of the above. In such systems, additional resource requirements become prohibitively expensive or simply impossible, therefore designs have to stay within prescribed constraints.

As in most engineering problems, the best solution is to compromise between the conflicting system properties with the dominant bound given an edge over the others. In extreme cases, the relative weight of some properties may be set to zero, ignoring everything except the primary design targets.

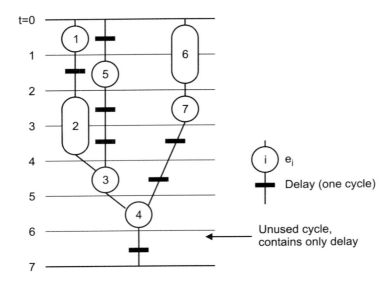

Figure 42   Visual representation of a scheduling plan

11.2   Initial allocation

After creating the graphical representation of a problem, one may estimate the
quality of possible solutions before scheduling. This estimation approximates
bounds to solutions (usually the quality of allocation) before scheduling the
graph. Estimating the quality of allocation is referred to as *initial allocation*.

During the creation of the system graph only the functions performed by
the operations are fixed. It is the responsibility of the designer to select the
physical properties of the processors. As the actual representation of hardware
capable of performing the desired function depends on system constraints,
selection of the module library must precede scheduling. A bit-serial multiplier
(slow, cheap, and simple) may be a better solution in flow-meter circuitry
than a parallel one (faster, more expensive, more silicon). On the other hand,
a parallel multiplier has the advantage of speed to be exploited in a PLC
(*programmable logic controller*, an embedded computer used in industrial
controls).

Choosing the module library fixes execution time for the elementary
operations as the capabilities of a given implementation are known. Having
a well-known module library also enables the designer to set up *operation
classes*, which contain operations types that may be realized in the same
processor.

As an example, addition and subtraction may be performed in the same kind of processor which is capable of signed operations. During scheduling, elementary operations performing addition and subtraction should be considered to utilize the same hardware resources. The *PIPE* design environment supports resource sharing by treating operation type (addition) and operation allocation type (add/subtract module) differently. After scheduling, it is the responsibility of the control hardware to supply the additional control signals required to implement multiple operation types.

After finding the module library, the EOG may be described using the time frame of its elementary operations. As the execution times of the operations are fixed by this step, a unique limit to the earliest and latest execution times of a given operation may be found. These times are called "As Soon As Possible" (ASAP) and "As Late As Possible" (ALAP) values. The ASAP value is the maximum of the length of data dependencies between the elementary operation and system inputs (considered to appear first at cycle 0). Similarly, the ALAP value is L minus the longest operation sequence between the operation and the system output. Operations may be started at any of the cycles between their ASAP and ALAP times, assuming none of their direct successors or predecessors have been started in conflicting cycles. See Figure 43.

As the control logic is non-ideal, additional safety features may be needed to guarantee proper execution. In the case of RESTART, the algorithm considers an operation started in cycle k with an execution time t_i to occupy one processor between cycles t_i and $t_i + k$ (inclusive). Some scheduling methods consider the operation to free its processor by cycle $t_i + k$, which requires more from implementation. This difference means that RESTART uses a safety margin of one cycle as an additional safety feature for tuning (RESTART requires less from the implementation of operations).

As ASAP and ALAP values are properties of the graph, they may be found based on data dependencies. The first and last possible starting cycle may change for an operation, depending on its predecessors and successors (i.e., inserting delay to the graph). This change of time frame may be expressed as change in the ASAP or ALAP values of the operation. It is feasible to introduce a set of current (actual) limit times, which are the actual boundaries of the time frame, and may differ from the absolute limits. *Soonest Limit Time* (SLT) and *Latest Limit Time* (LLT) are used to describe the actual properties (Figure 44). The limit times are bounded below by the ASAP and above by the ALAP values.

$$ASAP \leq SLT \leq LLT \leq ALAP$$

An operation with equal ASAP and ALAP values is blocked in its place, with no freedom. As such operations may not be moved without violating

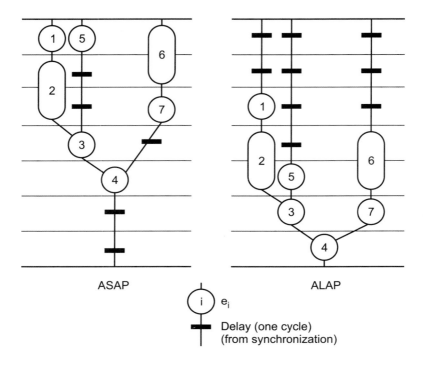

Figure 43   ALAP and ASAP values if $L = 7$

global timing constraints, they are not subject to scheduling. EOGs with operations that are all fixed are called *fixed graphs*. Since such graphs are impossible to improve by scheduling, fixed graphs are outside the scope of scheduling. (They are still subject to allocation.)

The operations with equal ASAP and ALAP values form the *critical transfer sequences* of the *critical path* of the graph. Inserting additional delay to these paths is impossible if the system is to be designed under a latency constraint and is already exhausted.

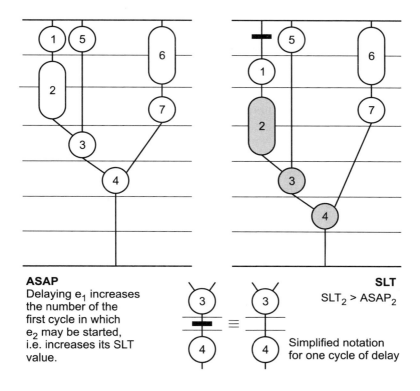

ASAP
Delaying e_1 increases the number of the first cycle in which e_2 may be started, i.e. increases its SLT value.

SLT
$SLT_2 > ASAP_2$

Simplified notation for one cycle of delay

Figure 44 ALAP and SLT

11.3 Initial approximation of the optimal solution

Even if the composition of an optimal scheduling plan is unknown, it may be possible to approximate the scheduling result of an optimal set of SLT and LLT values. Operation e_i requires at least q_i undisturbed cycles in a single processor for successful execution. (As e_i is truly elementary, there is no way to relocate the operation to a different processor once execution is started.) e_i is said to require q_i *load units* in type j_i processors for its realization.

By definition, one *load unit* is defined to be the usage of one processor's processing power in one cycle. As an operation always executes in one processor, its busy time introduces a load of q_i units altogether. (Note that q_i depends on the actual schedule. Details of this are covered later.) By adding the processor requirements of all operations in an EOG, a lower bound on the optimum resource usage may be given before scheduling. The total load of an EOG must be compared to the processing capacity offered by the processors in the system. A processor, when built, is available to suitable operations in the graph (those with an appropriate type) in all cycles, i.e., between cycles 0 and $R - 1$. A unit of processing power (*processing unit* for short) is defined as one processor being available for one cycle. N processors of a given type offer $N \cdot R$ processing units to be used by operations during R cycles. Dividing the number of load units by R gives the theoretical minimum of required processors.

The only uncertain item in load calculations is the effect of busy time. Since q_i depends on the relative timing of neighbouring operations, there is uncertainty about the difference between t_i and q_i. Considering q_i as the theoretical maximum is in most cases overly pessimistic, and therefore impractical.

Certain scheduling algorithms (notably hardware-constrained list scheduling) generate a solution that exactly matches the prescribed hardware utilization properties. The disadvantage is the increase of latency, which may be discovered only after scheduling. For these algorithms, an iterative process may be used that starts off with the optimal number of processors for all the processor types, relaxing the bound until the latency requirement is met.

Even if the number of simultaneously utilized processors is known before scheduling, allocation may increase the actual number of required processors. (This is caused by the requirement of pairwise compatibility during allocation, which may inhibit certain operations from being implemented in the same processor, even if their busy times do not necessarily overlap.) Certain integrated scheduling and allocation approaches (such as those described in [NP95]) model the effect of allocation during scheduling. The current version of the *PIPE* environment checks allocation only after scheduling.

11.4   Scheduling principles

Following initial allocation, the EOG scheduled may be described using a set of ASAP and ALAP values, descriptions of processor properties, and *operation classes*. A class of operations is a set of the elementary operation types that may be implemented in the same processor. The classes of operations depend on implementation technology.

A subtract operation, for example, may belong to the same class as a multiplication, if a general-purpose Arithmetic-Logic Unit (an *ALU*) is one of the possible processors. If the implementation has access to specialized modules, such as FPGA libraries, subtract and multiply operations are generally treated as different type operations. (The size and cost difference between specialized modules is considerable, if they are available.)

Solution of the scheduling problem removes any degree of freedom in time domain from the graph. The schedule prescribes a fixed starting time for every operation. This transformation strips any mobility from the elementary operations.

Since finding the optimal scheduling plan is unfortunately an NP-complete problem, suitable polynomial-time replacements are needed. Solution methods based on heuristics are used to achieve a scheduling plan near the optimum in less time. Note that most scheduling methods are not concerned with implementation details other than the number of required processors.

As an example, consider an EOG with a single long division operation. Assuming an execution time of $t_i = 24$ for division, a restart time of $R = 18$ may not be realized without replication. As described in Chapter 3, there should be two processors capable of dividing with $c_i = 2$. Scheduling, on the other hand, does not prescribe replication for the division elementary operation. As the number of processors is at least two (regardless of the actual schedule), and there is a single division inside the EOG, obviously such a system may be implemented only if the division operation is replicated ($c_i = 2$). Perceived this way, certain scheduling methods detect the need for processor replication without explicitly checking for it during RESTART.

Integer Linear Programming (ILP) based methods transform data dependencies and processor properties into linear systems of equalities and inequalities. Solution of these systems may be performed by an external solver package instead of internal resources.

ILP-based scheduling may handle pipelined execution. Most ILP-based schedulers generate very large numbers of equations even for problems of small to moderate sizes. Therefore, practical systems seldom rely on ILP-based solvers. As shown later, the most frequently used ILP description does not present an easy and efficient way of extending scheduling to consider busy time (q_i) instead of execution time (t_i) when finding idle cycles. For this reason, we consider ILP-based schedulers to be limited in scope, and they are not recommended for larger benchmark problems. ILP-based solutions are presented for comparison purposes only.

List scheduling is a collection of fast heuristics. Elementary operations are scheduled based on a *priority function*, with the operations that have the highest priority being scheduled before the others. A possible way to implement list scheduling is to scan time domain in increasing order, fix available operations that have the highest priorities and delay the scheduling of others. (Since time domain is scanned in increasing order, if an operation is fixed later, it is automatically started at a later cycle.)

The priority function is generally based on operation mobilities, with operations with lower mobility generally given precedence over those with more schedules. Operations are scheduled without look-ahead, therefore additional checks and iterations may be necessary after list scheduling.

List scheduling usually ignores any special properties of the data path (i.e., pipelined execution) and produces a fast solution of (usually) acceptable quality. Execution time is a low (up to second) order polynomial function of graph complexity. Extensions to handle busy time instead of execution time, pipelined execution, and operation type classes are available.

Force-directed scheduling is a scheduling method with a relatively high order (approximately third order) polynomial function of graph complexity. This algorithm schedules operations based on concurrence as a function of the utilization of individual processors. As a constant utilization minimizes idle time, force-directed scheduling tries to balance the number of concurrent operations with a cost function based on the deviation from the ideal concurrence. This cost function resembles the force exerted by springs based on Hooke's Law (hence the name force-directed). Force-directed scheduling is a modular method, easily modified to suit special needs. Possible options are optimization for bus width, transfer (memory), conditional branches and others. The extensions of force-directed scheduling that handle q_i instead of t_i are natural extensions of the algorithm.

11.5   Scheduling using Integer Linear Programming

A possible way to solve the scheduling problem is to transform data dependencies to sets of equalities and inequalities, which in turn may be solved by existing packages [HLH91]. Since a solver may be fine-tuned for ILP inequalities, an ILP-based scheduler needs to concentrate only on the scheduling problem itself. Variables in ILP inequalities are related to the starting times for the elementary operations, with other constants and variables representing external constraints.

Additional inequalities are used to make up data dependencies, inhibit time constraint violations, and define a cost function. In a given graph, after calculating the s_i ASAP and l_i ALAP times for elementary operations, all operations are assigned a number of binary variables, $x_{i,t}$, in such a way that $x_{i,t}$ is 1 if and only if the e_i is started in cycle t. The $x_{i,t}$ variables are equivalent to the start signals of processors. The number of processors of type j to be built into the system is M_j (operation e_i uses a processor of type j_i).

A maximum cost of D serves as an upper limit for realization. J is the number of different operation classes, with a weight of w_j belonging to processor type j. Weight values are relative values, presenting a way to describe the quality of a given solution.

As we permit different execution times for each of the elementary operations, elementary operation i started at cycle T ($x_{i,T} = 1$) requires at least t_i cycles to complete its task. For this reason, the processor in which

e_i is executing remains inaccessible for new data at least during cycles T to $T + t_i - 1$. Note that the actual busy time, q_i, is still not present in this description.

Sets of equations are constructed in the following way:

1. All elementary operations must start in their time frames:

$$1 = \sum_{t=s_i}^{l_i} x_{i,t} \quad (\forall i, 0 \le t < L)$$

   Trivial zero variables ($x_{i,t}$ outside operation time frame) are missing from ILP inequalities.

2. Processors executing operations remain inaccessible at least as long as the respective execution times. The $x'_{i,t}$ variables are non-zero in cycles where operations are executed.

$$x'_{i,t} = \begin{cases} 1 & \text{if } \exists x_{i,T} = 1 : t < T + t_i \\ 0 & \text{otherwise} \end{cases} \quad (0 \le t < L)$$

   Note that this notation does not describe busy time (q_i). In ILP models where execution times are treated as constants (such as the basic operation model in [HLH91]), no x' variables are defined.

3. Pipelined execution is represented by a set of auxiliary variables, $x''_{i,t}$. These variables represents the folded time domain, mapping $x'_{i,t}$ values that are concurrent in pipelined mode to the same x'':

$$x''_{i,t} = \sum_{j \equiv i[R]} x'_{j,t} \quad (0 \le t < R)$$

4. All operations are started in such a way that the number of simultaneously used processors of type j does not exceed M_j:

$$\left(\sum_{j_i=j} x''_{i,t} \right) - M_j \le 0 \quad (1 \le j \le J)$$

5. Data dependencies are not violated, so all operations are started at least t_i cycles before their direct successors. In other words, for every e_i and e_j pair such that $e_i \to e_j$

$$\left(\sum_{t=s_i}^{l_i} t x_{i,t} \right) - \left(\sum_{t=s_j}^{l_j} t x_{j,t} \right) < 0$$

As data dependencies are transitive, it is not necessary to set up inequalities for indirect connections.

6. Total cost of the system does not exceed its allowable maximum:

$$C = \sum_{j=1}^{J} w_j M_j \leq D$$

Rule (1) generates N equations, which is not changed by (2), since x and x' values have a one-to-one equivalence. Extending the equalities to pipelined mode (3) adds R equations by introducing new variables. Checking concurrence (4) adds $J \cdot R$ new inequalities. A data dependency inequality (5) is generated for each direct data transfer.

After generating ILP inequalities, the optimal solution (or one of the optimal solutions) must be found. This solution consists of binary numbers for $x_{i,t}$, which in turn prescribes the optimal starting time for operations. ILP-based scheduling depends on a special external tool to solve the sets of inequalities. While an external package may be highly optimized for the task, the time needed to find the optimal solution may not be predicted.

Since relations between start times of operations present nonlinear inequalities, the above ILP-based description may not be easily extended to concurrence based on q_i instead of t_i. Since q_i may depend on the relative timing of several operations (i.e., for each direct successor of e_i), the expression of q_i is defined as a maximum of several $q_{i,t}$ values, each defined by a different direct successor. (In fact, since the *max* operator is non-linear, traditional ILP solvers must be extended to handle q_i.)

An example of describing $q_{i,t}$ for e_i with a single direct successor e_j is:

$$q_{i,t} = x'_{i,t} + \max \left(\sum_{k=s_i}^{t-t_i} x_{i,k} x_{j,k+t_i}, x_{i,k+t_i} \right)$$

The first term denotes the possibility of e_i executing in cycle t. The first term in the sum describes cases where e_i and e_j are adjacent (i.e., $q_i = t_i + t_j$). The second sum term represents at least one additional cycle in $q_{i,t}$, which is implied by synchronization buffers before e_j, if applicable. (This additional cycle is extended further if the first sum term is present, which is covered by the max function.)

Unfortunately, the above description may not be solved with linear programming methods, and the number of additional equations gets large even with small N. Because of these problems, ILP-based solutions are not recommended for practical scheduling applications.

11.6   List scheduling

List scheduling is a collective name for simple methods using relatively small computational power. List scheduling is generally based on primitive priority functions. The total number of steps to perform list scheduling is proportional to the (at most) second power of system complexity. Elementary operations are put into a list based on their priority value, with the scheduling process scanning the time domain. Conflicts (resource contention caused by identical starting time for operations) are resolved based on the priority function, i.e., with the operations having lower priority being delayed (started later).

This delay is equivalent to a single cycle performed by a buffer. The main execution order of list scheduling is scanning in the time domain. For this reason, the algorithm works independently of the order of the elementary operations (unlike force-directed scheduling: see below). List scheduling requires a suitable priority function, based on operation mobility. The mapping of mobility to priority should be (strictly) monotonously decreasing so operations with a lower mobility are at an advantage during scheduling. Operation priority based on operation urgency is suitable.

A useful extension of list scheduling is the case of resource-bound list scheduling. This algorithm penalizes the violation of hardware cost constraints. A suitable priority function is based on a first-order decreasing function of mobility, with an upper limit set by operation concurrence. This composite function does not deal with a distribution not violating timing constraints while it penalizes the usage of additional hardware. An unfortunate disadvantage of resource-bound list scheduling is the iterative way of finding optimal hardware constraints (starting from the optimum requirements, increasing the synthesis target until fulfilling the latency condition).

List scheduling in itself does not involve analysis of pipelined structures. Multi-cycle operations may be scheduled using these algorithms, using a structure similar to look-ahead prediction. A possible solution of this problem is the introduction of a sufficiently long delay. This delay must be long enough so the placement of the delayed operation is not tried before the processor occupied by the winning operation is freed.

List scheduling, being the offspring of a simple function, is a very fast algorithm and terminates in a short time with a (usually) non-optimal solution. Compared to ILP-based scheduling, the total execution time may be approximated by an upper bound. The results received after list scheduling must be checked for activation and idle time, if optimal hardware requirements are not found before. As list scheduling presents a priority function based on local relations (i.e., mobilities), it produces a local optimum for all of the cycles, which in turn may yield non-optimal pipelined utilization.

11.6.1   General list scheduling

A typical list scheduling algorithm scans data propagation in the system
in time the domain. It requires the latency and a complete description of
the graph, calculates ASAP and ALAP times, and constructs the priority
function. The SLT and LLT values are started as ASAP and ALAP cycle
numbers. List scheduling simulates a straightforward method of delaying
operations, which is performed by fixing high-priority operations and delaying
others (i.e., increasing their SLT values). The scheduler itself runs a loop for
every cycle, finding operations that could be started in the current cycle. In
the case of competition, operations are given advantage in decreasing order
of priority. As this method starts with a fixed value of system latency, it is
suitable for scheduling systems operating under a latency constraint. Most
practical applications fall into this category. See Figure 45.

All the operations eligible for immediate start ("winners") are started (i.e.,
their SLT and LLT values are set to the current time value), while other
candidates ("losers") are delayed. This delay is performed by increasing their
SLT. A delayed operation has its priority function value increased as its LLT
time does not change (i.e., remains equal to the ALAP value) while delaying it
increases its SLT. As the priority function value is highest for the operations
with the lowest current mobility, a general list scheduling method preserves
the latency of the system. (It is impossible to win over an operation if it is
currently in its ALAP cycle, as it would require negative mobility.) Elementary
operations that are affected by delayed operations through a data dependency
are also subject to delay, therefore data dependency relations are not violated.
Checking pipelined utilization must be performed for systems operated in
overlapping mode. The local nature of the list scheduling does not enable the
scheduler to directly check for violations of hardware constraints in an easy
way. A possible solution is to employ back-tracking, but this makes the list
scheduler slower.

11.6.2   List scheduling under hardware constraint

Systems that are to be realized under a fixed cost of hardware components
may be scheduled using a modified type of list scheduling. Unlike general list
scheduling, this algorithm does not pre-set ALAP (and, therefore, LLT) values
of elementary operations, so total latency must be checked after fixing the last
operation. A Hardware-bound scheduling method scans cycles in increasing
order with the elementary operations checked for competition based on their
SLT times. Candidates are operations with their SLT values being equal to the
current cycle. As long as the number of candidates is lower than the processor
number constraint, they are all started in the current cycle. In the case of a

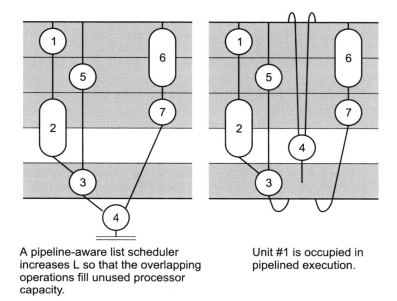

A pipeline-aware list scheduler increases L so that the overlapping operations fill unused processor capacity.

Unit #1 is occupied in pipelined execution.

Figure 45 List scheduling a pipelined structure

conflict (i.e., more candidates than available processor capacity), the excess must be delayed.

There are no generally useful rules to select the operations to be delayed, but a comparison of total execution times following a given operation may differentiate between candidates. An operation being followed by more operations may cause more problems if delayed, since it reduces the time frames of more operations than the other competitor. After scanning the data dependency graph the final value of latency may only be checked, but not modified. List scheduling is capable of finding an exact match for the prescribed hardware constraints if possible. A feasible balance between hardware costs and latency must be found. Due to the fast execution of list scheduling, an iterative application of the list scheduler is generally possible. As with the general list scheduling algorithm, list scheduling under a hardware constraint in its basic form is incapable of dealing with pipelined execution during the scheduling phase.

A typical application of hardware-constrained list scheduling is code generation for RISC-based processors. (Most state-of-the-art CISC processors employ similar speedup techniques, so they behave like RISC architecture microprocessors in this context.) Most RISC processors use an internal multiprocessor structure, i.e., instructions are fed to *execution units* (we use this name to avoid confusion with processor, which now refers to the RISC CPU itself). Execution units are the resources that must be properly utilized as they may work simultaneously.

11.7   Force-directed scheduling

Force-directed scheduling [PK89] is a modular scheduling algorithm, based on probabilistic approximations of utilization. It is based on the idea of balancing operation load in such a way that the difference between the maximum and minimum of concurrently used processors is small. Since the number of required processors is bounded below by the maximum of concurrently operating processors, the average utilization is large if the difference between maximum and minimum is small.

The deviation from the average utilization is weighted with the concurrent load in a way similar to Hooke's law ($F = -W\Delta W$). Force-directed scheduling minimizes a force-like function based on processor utilization, hence the name. Additional algorithmic extensions may be also introduced to the algorithm, usually as additive force terms. This flexibility, in addition to the good results achieved with force-directed scheduling, make this algorithm one of the most popular scheduling methods. Sometimes the algorithm serves as an example or as a special form of a benchmark. Force-directed scheduling is capable of dealing with optimization of both elementary operations and delays (i.e., buffers).

Force-directed scheduling is easy to describe if delay is not represented as buffers in the EOG. Delay effects are described by adjusting the starting time of operations, even if buffers will be introduced to the data path during implementation. Introducing buffers and moving them in the graph requires changes in data models. This modification also increases the number of elementary operations in the graph, which increases scheduling time. Therefore, we discuss force-directed scheduling as described in [PK89], i.e., without representing delay in the data path. (The effects of buffers are part of force-directed equations, but buffers are not represented in the EOG.)

The force function depends on a model of the resources needed by each elementary operation (elementary operation load). The load of an elementary operation is equal to the number of processors used during the execution of the operation, thus it is 1 for every time cycle in which the operation is active, for every fixed operation.

In the case of operations that have not been fixed, the load may be approximated. As the starting cycle of a moving operation is unknown, it may be approximated based on the operation's ASAP and ALAP times and the timing of its successors (since those influence busy time q_i). The approximation for each variable is to use a uniform probability function or every cycle of the available time frame.

The start probability function is defined so that $V_{i,t}$ is equal to the probability of starting elementary operation e_i in cycle t:

$$V_{i,t} = \begin{cases} \frac{1}{l_i - s_i + 1} & s_i \le t \le l_i \\ 0 & \text{otherwise} \end{cases}$$

The $V_{i,t}$ function is trivially extended to fixed operations, as it is equal to 1 for the starting cycle $t = s_i = l_i$.

As multicycle operations use a processor for every cycle in which they are operating, a function must be used to describe the actual load of elementary operations. The approximation of busy time is therefore defined as a conditional sum: $G_{i,t|k}$ is equal to the number of processors used by elementary operation e_i in cycle t, with the assumption that e_i is started in cycle k. Obviously,

$$G_{i,t|k} = \begin{cases} 1 & k \le t \le k + q_i - 1 \\ 0 & \text{otherwise} \end{cases}$$

Since the q_i in $G_{i,t|k}$ depends on the relative timing of e_i's direct successors, the actual function should approximate q_i.

1. For each fixed, direct successor of e_i, check if there is no chance for delay between the two operations. These successors each set a minimum for q_i:

$$\min q_i = \max_{j:e_i \to e_j} (t_i + t_j)$$

2. For each direct successor which may not start immediately after e_i finishes (because of other dependencies), synchronizing buffers are implied. Such buffers directly follow e_i, therefore their contribution to q_i is a single cycle:

$$\min q_i = t_i + 1$$

3. For each direct successor which is not yet fixed, there is uncertainty in the calculation of q_i itself. In this case, if one assumes that the start probability in each of the direct successors' available cycles is uniform, the data dependency implies synchronization buffers if $s_i + t_i < s_j$. The probability of this depends on the number of available cycles for e_j, which is $l_j - s_j + 1$. The difference between q_i and t_i is therefore approximated as

$$\min q_i = t_i + \begin{cases} 1 & \text{if } s_i + t_i < s_j \\ t_j & \text{otherwise} \end{cases}$$

Since the probability of $s_i + t_i = s_j$ is approximated as $1 - \frac{1}{l_j - s_j + 1}$, the value of q_i is at least 1 (i.e., the processor is busy at least in cycle $s_i + t_i$). In other cycles between $s_i + t_i + 1$ and $s_i + t_i + t_j$ (inclusive), the probability that the processor is busy in the given cycle (i.e., the cycle is part of q_i) is $\frac{1}{l_j - s_j + 1}$.

Since busy time must not be violated for any of the direct successors of e_i, the maximum of the above minimum values must be used as the approximated q_i.

The busy period of e_i is a function based on $V_{i,t}$ and $G_{i,t|k}$:

$$U_{i,t} = \sum_{t=0}^{L-1} G_{i,t|k} V_{i,k} \quad (s_i \leq k \leq l_i)$$

After finding busy times for each operation, operations of the same class must be totalled to find the utilization of processors as a function of time. $W_{j,t}$ is equal to the number of processors of type j used in cycle t (the *load function* for operations of type j).

$$W_{j,t} = \sum_{j_i=j} U_{i,t} = \sum_{j_i=j} \left(\sum_{t=0}^{L-1} G_{i,t|k} V_{i,k} \right) \quad (s_i \leq k \leq l_i, 0 \leq t < L)$$

During pipelined execution, cycles which are mapped to the same cycle in the range $0 \leq t < R$ happen simultaneously, so the load functions must be folded to reflect this. The folding process transforms the load in cycle t to cycle $(t \bmod R)$, where mod refers to the arithmetic modulo operator. (Using the notation of congruence, $t \equiv k[R]$ if $t \bmod R = k \bmod R$.) $C_{j,t}$ is equal to the number of processors of type j used in cycle t during pipelined execution, i.e., the overlapped load function of operations of type j as

$$C_{j,t} = \sum_{k \equiv t[R]} W_{j,k} \quad (0 \leq t < R, 0 \leq k < L)$$

For non-pipelined mode, obviously,

$$C_{j,t} = W_{j,t}$$

as $L = R$.

The number of type j processors to be built to the hardware unit may not be less than $\max\lceil C_{j,t} \rceil (0 \leq t < L)$. (Based on the efficiency of allocation, the actual requirement may be more, but never less.) A uniform load is desirable as it results in an overall high utilization and low idle percentage.

The force function describes the relative quantity of two scheduling plans with a higher force value denoting a solution of lower quality. The force value is defined between two schedules as

$$F_{C,\Delta C} = \sum_{j=1}^{J} w_j \left(\sum_{t=0}^{R-1} C_{0,j,t} \Delta C_{j,t} \right) = \sum_{j=1}^{J} w_j \left(\sum_{t=0}^{R-1} C_{0,j,t} (C_{j,t} - C_{0,j,t}) \right)$$

where $C_{j,t}$ refers to the overlapped load of the second (final) schedule, $C_{0,j,t}$ to the initial one. w_j is the relative cost of type j processors, as defined in Section 11.5. The notation

$$\Delta C_{j,t} = C_{j,t} - C_{0,j,t}$$

highlights the similarities between the above formula and Hooke's law.

A negative value of $F_{C,\Delta C}$ means a transition to a better scheduling plan.

A good starting cycle for an operation may be found by comparing the transition results from the initial, moving state to the states found after fixing the operation to every cycle in its time frame. The cycle resulting in the smallest $F_{C,\Delta C}$ value is chosen as the local optimum, after which the operation loses its mobility and is fixed to the optimal t cycle. Force-directed scheduling scans all of the moving elements, finding the minimum of F for all of their possible starting cycles. As the best one is found, the element is fixed there, and the next element is scheduled.

As force-directed scheduling scans the elementary operations sequentially, it is not immune to the effects of ordering the operations (transitions to local optima do not always end in a global optimum). A typical example of that is the so-called *"bottleneck"*, an operation with multiple inputs and, serving multiple operation, separating the graph (Figure 46). Premature scheduling of a bottleneck operation may result in a disaster for other operations as it reduces the time frames for a lot of operations.

As force-directed scheduling has an execution time of an approximately third order function of system complexity, it executes much more slowly than list scheduling.

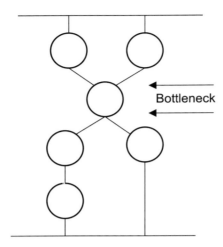

Figure 46   Section of a graph containing a bottleneck

11.8   Special problems of conditional execution

Elementary operation graphs may contain parallel branches that are executed if and only if an expression is valid. Presence of such a branch is a serious problem during scheduling as conditional execution may be treated as a static (worst-case) problem or using a heuristic model (which requires statistical information on data processed by the hardware). Choosing the model of the conditional execution is not easy as both methods are useful only under certain conditions.

Worst-case models of conditional execution prescribe the system to be able to handle any sequence of inputs without decreasing performance. This condition during scheduling requires the scheduler to find the worst-case input sequence and find a hardware structure that is capable of dealing with the problem. Worst-case design is usually an overestimation of system load and increases realization costs due to the additional resources which must be available.

The worst-case model of the conditional branches treats the branches as if they were executing always fully parallel (requiring the maximum of resources the branches need in a given cycle). A system designed to deal with such a load would be able to execute all possible inputs with the same latency. This property, however, means that some of the built-in processors would not be used most of the time.

The opposite of worst-case design is a probability-based method of conditional execution. This approximation presents a model of conditional execution that needs knowledge of the distribution for input values. The conditional branches are given weight values depending on the probability of execution in the mutually exclusive branches. The condition at the beginning of the branches is said to take the branches with a similar distribution. After this step, throughput depends on the inputs following this distribution; data that deviates may slow down the system.

A typical usage of probability-based conditional execution is the internal structure of RISC processors. Such a processor features different types of execution units, each capable of dealing with a given set of instructions. Instructions executed inside the processor enter one of the units depending on the type of operation they perform. As an example, a PowerPC 604 may fetch four instructions in a single clock cycle; worst-case design would suggest a minimum of four pieces of all execution units (more for multi-cycle types). The designers of the PowerPC 604 chose to reduce the number of units to one in all types except single-cycle integer operations (which are built twice). This implementation means that the PowerPC 604 keeps on running at maximum speed (starting the execution of four instructions every clock cycle) if the instructions may be dispatched without stalls. As the number of units is lower than the worst-case value, the processor may encounter instructions that may not be dispatched to the respective units as they are still processing the previous instruction. This situation (a data overrun or stall) prevents execution of instructions and results in idle clock cycles for the processor. As a black box, the processor may be modelled as an execution unit that executes instructions with a speed that does not depend on the input sequence. This property is a disadvantage if the method is compared to worst-case design (as it changes the characteristics of the elementary operations).

12

Examples for comparison of the scheduling algorithms

For comparison of different scheduling algorithms, we use the same problem graph (Figure 47). During scheduling the pipelined execution mode is also used, with a restart time of five cycles.

Our system is operating in an environment such that latency must be equal to or less than 7. This is equivalent to $l_4 \leq 6$. (This constraint prescribes L to be less than 8, and is set by the external units connected to our device. Any solution resulting in L greater than 7 must be discarded as it ruins the timing for the environment. A latency value below 8 is suitable, probably extended to 7 using inserted delay elements.)

We distinguish between two different processors, one used for executing single-cycle operations, the other for multiple-cycle execution. The cost of single-cycle (type 1) processors is one-half of the cost of multi-cycle (type 2) processors ($w_1 = 1, w_2 = 2$).

12.1 ILP solution inequalities

The respective cost for processors is proportional to the execution time, i.e., $w_1 = 1$ and $w_2 = 2$. The total system cost must be kept under $D = 12$. The number of processors is M_1 and M_2; the total implementation cost is

$$C = w_1 \cdot M_1 + w_2 \cdot M_2 = M_1 + 2 \cdot M_2$$

As discussed in Chapter 11, the ILP inequalities are not extended to handle busy times (q_i) instead of t_i because of limitations in ILP-based scheduling methods.

Operation i	ASAP s_i	ALAP l_i	type j_i	execution time t_i
1	0	2	1	1
2	1	3	2	2
3	3	5	1	1
4	4	6	1	1
5	0	4	1	1
6	0	3	2	2
7	2	5	1	1

Non-trivial starting time variables $(x_{i,t})$ are found based on the ASAP and ALAP values:

t	$x_{1,t}$	$x_{2,t}$	$x_{3,t}$	$x_{4,t}$	$x_{5,t}$	$x_{6,t}$	$x_{7,t}$
0	$x_{1,0}$	0	0	0	$x_{5,0}$	$x_{6,0}$	0
1	$x_{1,1}$	$x_{2,1}$	0	0	$x_{5,1}$	$x_{6,1}$	0
2	$x_{1,2}$	$x_{2,2}$	0	0	$x_{5,2}$	$x_{6,2}$	$x_{7,2}$
3	0	$x_{2,3}$	$x_{3,3}$	0	$x_{5,3}$	$x_{6,3}$	$x_{7,3}$
4	0	0	$x_{3,4}$	$x_{4,4}$	$x_{5,4}$	0	$x_{7,4}$
5	0	0	$x_{3,5}$	$x_{4,5}$	0	0	$x_{7,5}$
6	0	0	0	$x_{4,6}$	0	0	0

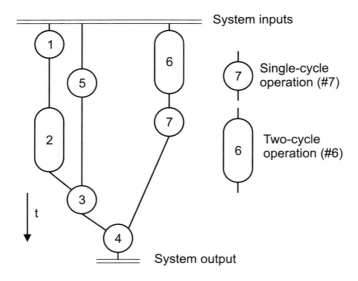

Figure 47   An EOG for comparison of scheduling algorithms

As there are multiple-cycle operations present, they use their processors during both their first and second cycles. For this reason, the number of processors used in the implementation of such an operation is expressed by $x'_{i,t}$:

t	j : single-cycle operations $x'_{j,t}$	$x'_{2,t}$	$x'_{6,t}$
0	$x_{j,0}$	0	$x_{6,0}$
1	$x_{j,1}$	$x_{2,1}$	$x_{6,1} + x_{6,0}$
2	$x_{j,2}$	$x_{2,2} + x_{2,1}$	$x_{6,2} + x_{6,1}$
3	$x_{j,3}$	$x_{2,3} + x_{2,2}$	$x_{6,3} + x_{6,2}$
4	$x_{j,4}$	$x_{2,3}$	$x_{6,3}$
5	$x_{j,5}$	0	0
6	$x_{j,6}$	0	0

For a pipelined execution mode with $R = 5$, the sixth cycle executes simultaneously with cycle 0 of the next data. This is also true for the seventh and first cycles, so this pipelined utilization is found by folding the table, and generating the $x''_{i,t}$ variables in the process:

$$x''_{i,0} = x'_{i,0} + x'_{i,5}$$
$$x''_{i,1} = x'_{i,1} + x'_{i,7}$$

t	j : single-cycle operations $x''_{j,t}$	$x''_{2,t}$	$x''_{6,t}$
0	$x_{j,0} + x_{j,5}$	0	$x_{6,0}$
1	$x_{j,1} + x_{j,6}$	$x_{2,1}$	$x_{6,1} + x_{6,0}$
2	$x_{j,2}$	$x_{2,2} + x_{2,1}$	$x_{6,2} + x_{6,1}$
3	$x_{j,3}$	$x_{2,3} + x_{2,2}$	$x_{6,3} + x_{6,2}$
4	$x_{j,4}$	$x_{2,3}$	$x_{6,3}$

During the generation of $x_{i,t}$ values, we have already discarded trivial zero variables. $x_{1,6}$ is an example as the ALAP time of operation e_1 (2) is less than 6. As every operation must start in a cycle between its ASAP and ALAP time, the following equalities hold:

$$x_{1,0} + x_{1,1} + x_{1,2} = 1$$
$$x_{2,1} + x_{2,2} + x_{2,3} = 1$$
$$x_{3,3} + x_{3,4} + x_{3,5} = 1$$
$$x_{4,4} + x_{4,5} + x_{4,6} = 1$$
$$x_{5,0} + x_{5,1} + x_{5,2} + x_{5,3} + x_{5,4} = 1$$
$$x_{6,0} + x_{6,1} + x_{6,2} + x_{6,3} = 1$$
$$x_{7,2} + x_{7,3} + x_{7,4} + x_{7,5} = 1$$

The total number of built-in processors must be sufficient to execute all of the operations. We distinguish between the pipelined and non-pipelined execution mode:

1. Non-overlapping execution, no wrapping in time domain:

   As there are multicycle operations, the number of concurrently used processors is based on $x'_{i,t}$. As the external system solves our inequalities for $x_{i,t}$, it is useful to substitute $x_{i,t}$ immediately. The total of simultaneously utilized processors must be found for every T such that $0 \leq t \leq L - 1$:

$$x_{1,0} + x_{5,0} - M_1 \leq 0$$
$$x_{1,1} + x_{5,1} - M_1 \leq 0$$
$$x_{1,2} + x_{5,2} + x_{7,2} - M_1 \leq 0$$
$$x_{3,3} + x_{5,3} + x_{7,3} - M_1 \leq 0$$
$$x_{3,4} + x_{5,4} + x_{7,4} - M_1 \leq 0$$
$$x_{3,5} + x_{4,5} + x_{7,5} - M_1 \leq 0$$
$$x_{4,6} - M_1 \leq 0$$

$$x_{6,0} - M_2 \leq 0$$
$$x_{2,1} + x_{6,1} + x_{6,0} - M_2 \leq 0$$
$$\text{(as } x'_{2,1} = x_{2,1} \text{ and } x'_{6,1} = x_{6,0} + x_{6,1})$$
$$x_{2,2} + x_{2,1} + x_{6,2} + x_{6,1} - M_2 \leq 0$$
$$x_{2,3} + x_{2,2} + x_{6,3} + x_{6,2} - M_2 \leq 0$$
$$x_{2,3} + x_{6,3} - M_2 \leq 0$$

The trivial lines (i.e., for $t = 5 : 0 - M_2 \leq 0$) are omitted.

2. Pipelined execution, time domain is folded:

In addition to multicycle operations, system time must be folded to reflect the overlapping execution, so we need the overlapping $x''_{i,t}$ values. The total of simultaneously utilized processors must be found for every T such that $0 \le t \le R - 1$:

$$x_{1,0} + x_{5,0} + x_{3,5} + x_{4,5} + x_{7,5} - M_1 \le 0$$
$$x_{1,1} + x_{5,1} + x_{4,6} - M_1 \le 0$$
$$x_{1,2} + x_{5,2} + x_{7,2} - M_1 \le 0$$
$$x_{3,3} + x_{5,3} + x_{7,3} - M_1 \le 0$$
$$x_{3,4} + x_{5,4} + x_{7,4} - M_1 \le 0$$

as

$$x''_{4,0} = x_{4,0} + x_{4,5} = x_{4,5}$$
$$x''_{3,0} = x_{3,0} + x_{3,5} = x_{3,5}$$
$$x''_{7,0} = x_{7,0} + x_{7,5} = x_{7,5}$$
$$x''_{4,1} = x_{4,1} + x_{4,6} = x_{4,6}$$
$$x''_{3,1} = x_{3,1} + x_{3,6} = 0$$
$$x''_{7,1} = x_{7,1} + x_{7,6} = 0$$

Other operations (e.g. e_1) are unaffected because of their ALAP times: $l_1 \le R - 1$, so that e_1 may never occupy a processor after cycle R.

$$x_{6,0} - M_2 \le 0$$
$$x_{2,1} + x_{6,1} + x_{6,0} - M_2 \le 0$$
$$x_{2,2} + x_{2,1} + x_{6,2} + x_{6,1} - M_2 \le 0$$
$$x_{2,3} + x_{2,2} + x_{6,3} + x_{6,2} - M_2 \le 0$$
$$x_{2,3} + x_{6,3} - M_2 \le 0$$

(Note that because of the ASAP and ALAP times of e_2 and e_6, the folding of inequalities did not affect the system for operations of type 2.)

3. Data dependencies must not be violated. This prescribes the following relations:

$$e_1 \rightarrow e_2, \quad e_2 \rightarrow e_3$$
$$e_3 \rightarrow e_4, \quad e_5 \rightarrow e_3$$
$$e_6 \rightarrow e_7, \quad e_7 \rightarrow e_4$$

Note that the following indirect dependencies are not used:

$$e_1 \nrightarrow e_3, \quad e_1 \nrightarrow e_4$$
$$e_5 \nrightarrow e_4, \quad e_6 \nrightarrow e_4$$

(They result in a number of redundant inequalities.)

$$0 \cdot x_{1,0} + 1 \cdot x_{1,1} + 2 \cdot x_{1,2} - 1 \cdot x_{2,1} - 2 \cdot x_{2,2} - 3 \cdot x_{2,3} \leq -1$$
$$1 \cdot x_{2,1} + 2 \cdot x_{2,2} + 3 \cdot x_{2,3} - 3 \cdot x_{3,3} - 4 \cdot x_{3,4} - 5 \cdot x_{3,5} \leq -1$$
$$3 \cdot x_{3,3} + 4 \cdot x_{3,4} + 5 \cdot x_{3,5} - 4 \cdot x_{4,4} - 5 \cdot x_{4,5} - 6 \cdot x_{4,6} \leq -1$$
$$0 \cdot x_{5,0} + 1 \cdot x_{5,1} + 2 \cdot x_{5,2} + 4 \cdot x_{5,4} - 3 \cdot x_{3,3} - 4 \cdot x_{3,4} - 5 \cdot x_{3,5} \leq -1$$
$$0 \cdot x_{6,0} + 1 \cdot x_{6,1} + 2 \cdot x_{6,2} + 3 \cdot x_{6,3} - 2 \cdot x_{7,2} - 3 \cdot x_{7,3} - 4 \cdot x_{7,4} - 5 \cdot x_{7,5} \leq -1$$
$$2 \cdot x_{7,2} + 3 \cdot x_{7,3} + 4 \cdot x_{7,4} + 5 \cdot x_{7,5} - 4 \cdot x_{4,4} - 5 \cdot x_{4,5} - 6 \cdot x_{4,6} \leq -1$$

The redundancy of the $e_1 \rightarrow e_3$ dependency is clear as it is equivalent to the sum of the $e_1 \rightarrow e_2$ and $e_2 \rightarrow e_3$ inequalities.

4. The total implementation cost must be kept below the cost limit:

$$C = M_1 + 2 \cdot M_2 \leq D$$
$$D = 12.$$

Solutions minimize C. A possible solution is the following:

1. Non-pipelined execution:

$$x_{1,0} = x_{2,1} = x_{3,3} = x_{4,6} = x_{5,1} = x_{6,3} = x_{7,4} = 1$$
$$M_1 = M_2 = 1$$
$$C = 3 \leq D$$

2. Pipelined execution:

$$x_{1,0} = x_{2,2} = x_{3,4} = x_{4,6} = x_{5,3} = x_{6,0} = x_{7,3} = 1$$
$$M_1 = M_2 = 1$$
$$C = 3 \leq D$$

12.2 List scheduling solutions

Our system is operating in an environment such that latency must be equal to or less than 7. This is equivalent to $l_4 \leq 6$. We distinguish between two different processors, one used for executing single-cycle operations, the other for multiple-cycle execution.

The number of processors (M_1 and M_2) must be minimized. The priority (p_i) is equal to $4 - (l_i - s_i + 1)$; operations with a lower priority value are at a disadvantage.

Operation i	ASAP s_i	ALAP l_i	type j_i	mobility m_i
1	0	2	1	3
2	1	3	2	3
3	3	5	1	3
4	4	6	1	3
5	0	4	1	5
6	0	3	2	4
7	2	5	1	4

The time domain is scanned in increasing order as follows.

Cycle 0: Competition between e_1 and e_5. As $p_1 = 2 > p_5 = 0$, e_5 is delayed; this affects no other operation as e_5 was not in its ALAP cycle. The winner, e_1, is fixed so $s_1 = l_1 = 0$. e_6 is fixed without competition as there is no other operation of type 2 that may be started in $t = 0$.

i	s_i	l_i	m_i
1	0	0	0
2	1	3	2
3	3	5	2
4	4	6	2
5	1	4	3
6	0	0	0
7	2	5	3

Cycle 1: No competition; e_2 and e_5 are started.

i	s_i	l_i	m_i
1	0	0	0
2	1	1	0
3	3	5	2
4	4	6	2
5	1	1	0
6	0	0	0
7	2	5	3

Cycles 2, 3 and 4: e_7, e_3 and e_4 are fixed without competition.

i	s_i	l_i	m_i
1	0	0	0
2	1	1	0
3	2	2	0
4	2	2	0
5	1	1	0
6	0	0	0
7	2	2	0

Cycles 5 and 6: No operations remain to be scheduled for these cycles.

The final result is:

i	s_i	l_i	m_i
1	0	0	0
2	1	1	0
3	2	2	0
4	2	2	0
5	1	1	0
6	0	0	0
7	2	2	0

This scheduling plan requires one unit of type 1 and two units of type 2 as the second cycle of e_6 is operating simultaneously with the first cycle of e_2, which requires more processors than the optimal solution $M_2 = 1$. Total latency is 5. (This may be extended to 7 by inserting a delay of *two* cycles somewhere, if latency should be exactly 7. This is a decision that must be made judging the properties of the environment.)

Should the system be operated with a restart time of 5, there would be no change in the number of processors required as $L = 5$ is equal to $R = 5$. (Therefore, there is no difference between pipelined and non-pipelined execution.)

12.3 List scheduling under hardware constraint

Our system is operating in an environment such that only one processor is available for type 1 and one for type 2 ($M_1 = M_2 = 1$). The system latency must be found.

The priority (p_i) is equal to the total execution time for operations following e_i. Operations with a lower priority value are at a disadvantage.

The time domain is scanned in increasing order, as follows.

Cycle 0: Competition between e_1 and e_5. As $p_1 = 4 > p_5 = 2$, e_5 is delayed. The winner, e_1, is fixed so $s_1 = l_1 = 0$. e_6 is fixed without competition as there is no other operation of type 2 that may be started in $t = 0$.

Cycle 1: e_5 is started. e_2 may not be started as the only available type 2 is in its second cycle. Delaying e_2 increases s_3 and s_4 due to data dependencies.

Cycle 2: e_2 and e_7 are started. There is no competition.

Cycle 3: No operation is started as there is no $s_i = 3$ value in the table.

Cycle 4: and

Cycle 5: e_3 and e_4 are started without competition.

The final result is that this scheduling plan requires one processor of type 1 and one of type 2, as prescribed. Latency, however, is increased to 6.

Pipelined execution with a restart time of 5 violates system constraints, as e_4 is started in $t = 5$, e_1 in $t = 0$, which cycles happen simultaneously. This results in a collision of data if a single processor is used for e_1 and e_4. A pipeline-aware list scheduler would delay e_4 so that it would be "folded" to an empty cycle of the $0 \ldots R - 1$ range. The first unoccupied cycle would be $t = 8$ (equivalent to $t = 3$), so e_4 would be fixed to $s_4 = 8$. This increases latency to $L = 9$.

12.4 Force-directed solutions

To calculate the functions of the force-directed scheduling, we use a common denominator of 60, so most of the calculations are transformed to integers.

12.4.1   Non-pipeline solution based on t_i

i	s_i	l_i	j_i	t_i	$V_{i,0}$	$V_{i,1}$	$V_{i,2}$	$V_{i,3}$	$V_{i,4}$	$V_{i,5}$	$V_{i,6}$
1	0	2	1	1	20/60	20/60	20/60				
2	1	3	2	2		20/60	20/60	20/60			
3	3	5	1	1				20/60	20/60	20/60	
4	4	6	1	1					20/60	20/60	20/60
5	0	4	1	1	12/60	12/60	12/60	12/60	12/60		
6	0	3	2	2	15/60	15/60	15/60	15/60			
7	2	5	1	1			15/60	15/60	15/60	15/60	

As there are multi-cycle operations in the graph, $U_{i,t}$ must be adjusted to reflect this. For other operations, $U_{i,t} = V_{i,t}$. $C_{j,t} \equiv W_{j,t}$ as there is no overlapping in the time domain.

i	s_i	l_i	j_i	t_i	$U_{i,0}$	$U_{i,1}$	$U_{i,2}$	$U_{i,3}$	$U_{i,4}$	$U_{i,5}$	$U_{i,6}$
1	0	2	1	1	20/60	20/60	20/60				
2	1	3	2	2		20/60	40/60	40/60	20/60		
3	3	5	1	1				20/60	20/60	20/60	
4	4	6	1	1					20/60	20/60	20/60
5	0	4	1	1	12/60	12/60	12/60	12/60	12/60		
6	0	3	2	2	15/60	30/60	30/60	30/60	15/60		
7	2	5	1	1			15/60	15/60	15/60	15/60	
$C_{0,1,t}$					32/60	32/60	47/60	47/60	67/60	55/60	20/60
$C_{0,2,t}$					15/60	50/60	70/60	70/60	35/60	0	0

We find the optimal starting cycle for e_1 first. Cycles are scanned in increasing direction, from $s_1 = 0$ to $l_1 = 2$.

Fixing e_1 to cycle 0 yields

i	s_i	l_i	j_i	t_i	$U_{i,0}$	$U_{i,1}$	$U_{i,2}$	$U_{i,3}$	$U_{i,4}$	$U_{i,5}$	$U_{i,6}$
1	0	0	1	1	60/60						
2	1	3	2	2		20/60	40/60	40/60	20/60		
3	3	5	1	1				20/60	20/60	20/60	
4	4	6	1	1					20/60	20/60	20/60
5	0	4	1	1	12/60	12/60	12/60	12/60	12/60		
6	0	3	2	2	15/60	30/60	30/60	30/60	15/60		
7	2	5	1	1			15/60	15/60	15/60	15/60	
$C_{0,1,t}$					32/60	32/60	47/60	47/60	67/60	55/60	20/60
$C_{0,2,t}$					15/60	50/60	70/60	70/60	35/60	0	0
$C_{1,t}$					72/60	12/60	27/60	47/60	67/60	55/60	20/60
$C_{2,t}$					15/60	50/60	70/60	70/60	35/60	0	0
$\Delta C_{1,t}$					+40/60	−20/60	−20/60	0	0	0	0
$\Delta C_{2,t}$					0	0	0	0	0	0	0

$C_{0,i,t}$ denotes the initial, $C_{i,t}$ the adjusted (final) C values; the difference is $\Delta C_{i,t} = C_{i,t} - C_{0,i,t}$:

$$F_{C,\Delta C} = \frac{32 \cdot 40 - 32 \cdot 20 - 47 \cdot 20}{3600} = -\frac{300}{3600}$$

The negative sign means an improvement of the initial schedule.

Fixing e_1 to cycle 1 results in

i	s_i	l_i	j_i	t_i	$U_{i,0}$	$U_{i,1}$	$U_{i,2}$	$U_{i,3}$	$U_{i,4}$	$U_{i,5}$	$U_{i,6}$
1	1	1	1	1		60/60					
2	2	3	2	2			30/60	60/60	30/60		
3	4	5	1	1					30/60	30/60	
4	5	6	1	1						30/60	30/60
5	0	4	1	1	12/60	12/60	12/60	12/60	12/60		
6	0	3	2	2	15/60	30/60	30/60	30/60	15/60		
7	2	5	1	1			15/60	15/60	15/60	15/60	
			$C_{0,1,t}$		32/60	32/60	47/60	47/60	67/60	55/60	20/60
			$C_{0,2,t}$		15/60	50/60	70/60	70/60	35/60	0	0
			$C_{1,t}$		12/60	72/60	27/60	47/60	67/60	75/60	30/60
			$C_{2,t}$		15/60	30/60	60/60	90/60	45/60	0	0
			$\Delta C_{1,t}$		−20/60	40/60	−20/60	−20/60	−10/60	20/60	10/60
			$\Delta C_{2,t}$		0	−20/60	−10/60	20/60	10/60	0	0

$$
\begin{aligned}
F_{C,\Delta C} &= \frac{2 \cdot (-50 \cdot 20 - 70 \cdot 10 + 70 \cdot 20 + 35 \cdot 10)}{3600} \\
&\quad + \frac{-32 \cdot 20 + 32 \cdot 40 - 47 \cdot 20 - 47 \cdot 20 - 67 \cdot 10 + 55 \cdot 20 + 20 \cdot 10}{3600} \\
&= -\frac{510}{3600}
\end{aligned}
$$

Fixing e_1 to cycle 2 causes

i	s_i	l_i	j_i	t_i	$U_{i,0}$	$U_{i,1}$	$U_{i,2}$	$U_{i,3}$	$U_{i,4}$	$U_{i,5}$	$U_{i,6}$
1	2	2	1	1			60/60				
2	3	3	2	2				60/60	60/60		
3	5	5	1	1						60/60	
4	6	6	1	1							60/60
5	0	4	1	1	12/60	12/60	12/60	12/60	12/60		
6	0	3	2	2	15/60	30/60	30/60	30/60	15/30		
7	2	5	1	1			15/60	15/60	15/60	15/60	
			$C_{0,1,t}$		32/60	32/60	47/60	47/60	67/60	55/60	20/60
			$C_{0,2,t}$		15/60	50/60	70/60	70/60	35/60	0	0
			$C_{1,t}$		12/60	12/60	87/60	27/60	27/60	75/60	60/60
			$C_{2,t}$		15/60	30/60	30/60	90/60	75/60	0	0
			$\Delta C_{1,t}$		−20/60	−20/60	+40/60	−20/60	−40/60	+20/60	+40/60
			$\Delta C_{2,t}$		0	−20/60	−40/60	+20/60	40/60	0	0

$$F_{C,\Delta C} = 2 \cdot \frac{-50 \cdot 20 - 40 \cdot 70 + 20 \cdot 70 + 40 \cdot 35}{3600}$$
$$+ \frac{-20 \cdot 32 - 20 \cdot 32 + 40 \cdot 47 - 20 \cdot 47 - 40 \cdot 67 + 20 \cdot 55 + 40 \cdot 20}{3600}$$
$$= -\frac{3120}{3600}$$

As $F_{C,\Delta C}$ had its minimum when e_1 was fixed to cycle 2, this position is the initial scheduling plan for the next operation. Note that the successors of e_1 are also fixed as e_1 is started in its ALAP cycle:

i	s_i	l_i	j_i	t_i	$U_{i,0}$	$U_{i,1}$	$U_{i,2}$	$U_{i,3}$	$U_{i,4}$	$U_{i,5}$	$U_{i,6}$
1	2	2	1	1			60/60				
2	3	3	2	2				60/60	60/60		
3	5	5	1	1						60/60	
4	6	6	1	1							60/60
5	0	4	1	1	12/60	12/60	12/60	12/60	12/60		
6	0	3	2	2	15/60	30/60	30/60	30/60	15/30		
7	2	5	1	1			15/60	15/60	15/60	15/60	
				$C_{1,t}$	12/60	12/60	87/60	27/60	27/60	75/60	60/60
				$C_{2,t}$	15/60	30/60	30/60	90/60	75/60	0	0

The next operation to schedule is e_6. The time domain is scanned in increasing order, from cycle 0 to cycle 3. As we fix e_6 to cycle 0:

i	s_i	l_i	j_i	t_i	$U_{i,0}$	$U_{i,1}$	$U_{i,2}$	$U_{i,3}$	$U_{i,4}$	$U_{i,5}$	$U_{i,6}$
1	2	2	1	1			60/60				
2	3	3	2	2				60/60	60/60		
3	5	5	1	1						60/60	
4	6	6	1	1							60/60
5	0	4	1	1	12/60	12/60	12/60	12/60	12/60		
6	0	0	2	2	60/60	60/60					
7	2	5	1	1			15/60	15/60	15/60	15/60	
				$C_{0,1,t}$	12/60	12/60	87/60	27/60	27/60	75/60	60/60
				$C_{0,2,t}$	15/60	30/60	30/60	90/60	75/60	0	0
				$C_{1,t}$	12/60	12/60	87/60	27/60	27/60	75/60	60/60
				$C_{2,t}$	60/60	60/60	0	60/60	60/60	0	0
				$\Delta C_{1,t}$	0	0	0	0	0	0	0
				$\Delta C_{2,t}$	+45/60	+30/60	−30/60	−30/60	−15/60	0	0

$$F_{C,\Delta C} = 2 \cdot \frac{45 \cdot 15 + 30 \cdot 30 - 30 \cdot 30 - 30 \cdot 90 - 15 \cdot 75}{3600} = -\frac{6300}{3600}$$

Setting cycle 1 as starting time for e_6 yields

i	s_i	l_i	j_i	t_i	$U_{i,0}$	$U_{i,1}$	$U_{i,2}$	$U_{i,3}$	$U_{i,4}$	$U_{i,5}$	$U_{i,6}$
1	2	2	1	1			60/60				
2	3	3	2	2				60/60	60/60		
3	5	5	1	1						60/60	
4	6	6	1	1							60/60
5	0	4	1	1	12/60	12/60	12/60	12/60	12/60		
6	1	1	2	2		60/60	60/60				
7	3	5	1	1				20/60	20/60	20/60	
				$C_{0,1,t}$	12/60	12/60	87/60	27/60	27/60	75/60	60/60
				$C_{0,2,t}$	15/60	30/60	30/60	90/60	75/60	0	0
				$C_{1,t}$	12/60	12/60	72/60	32/60	32/60	85/60	60/60
				$C_{2,t}$	0	60/60	60/60	60/60	60/60	0	0
				$\Delta C_{1,t}$	0	0	−15/60	+5/60	+5/60	+5/60	0
				$\Delta C_{2,t}$	−15/60	+30/60	+30/60	−30/60	−15/60	0	0

$$
\begin{aligned}
F_{C,\Delta C} &= 2 \cdot \frac{-15 \cdot 15 - 30 \cdot 30 + 30 \cdot 30 + 30 \cdot 90 - 15 \cdot 75}{3600} \\
&\quad + \frac{-15 \cdot 87 - 15 \cdot 27 + 15 \cdot 27 + 15 \cdot 75}{3600} \\
&= -\frac{5160}{3600}
\end{aligned}
$$

Setting $s_6 = l_6 = 1$ results in

i	s_i	l_i	j_i	t_i	$U_{i,0}$	$U_{i,1}$	$U_{i,2}$	$U_{i,3}$	$U_{i,4}$	$U_{i,5}$	$U_{i,6}$
1	2	2	1	1			60/60				
2	3	3	2	2				60/60	60/60		
3	5	5	1	1						60/60	
4	6	6	1	1							60/60
5	0	4	1	1	12/60	12/60	12/60	12/60	12/60		
6	2	2	2	2			60/60	60/60			
7	4	5	1	1					30/60	30/60	
				$C_{0,1,t}$	12/60	12/60	87/60	27/60	27/60	75/60	60/60
				$C_{0,2,t}$	15/60	30/60	30/60	90/60	75/60	0	0
				$C_{1,t}$	12/60	12/60	72/60	12/60	42/60	95/60	60/60
				$C_{2,t}$	0	0	60/60	120/60	60/60	0	0
				$\Delta C_{1,t}$	0	0	−15/60	−15/60	15/60	15/60	0
				$\Delta C_{2,t}$	−15/60	−30/60	30/60	30/60	−15/60	0	0

$$
\begin{aligned}
F_{C,\Delta C} &= 2 \cdot \frac{-15 \cdot 15 - 30 \cdot 30 + 30 \cdot 30 + 30 \cdot 90 - 15 \cdot 75}{3600} \\
&\quad + \frac{-15 \cdot 87 - 15 \cdot 27 + 15 \cdot 27 + 15 \cdot 75}{3600} \\
&= \frac{2520}{3600}
\end{aligned}
$$

Note that this large positive value means a definite change in quality, as the new schedule requires *two* type 2 processors due to $C_{2,3} = 2$.

Starting e_6 in cycle 3 produces a similar collision in cycles 3 and 4:

i	s_i	l_i	j_i	t_i	$U_{i,0}$	$U_{i,1}$	$U_{i,2}$	$U_{i,3}$	$U_{i,4}$	$U_{i,5}$	$U_{i,6}$
1	2	2	1	1			60/60				
2	3	3	2	2				60/60	60/60		
3	5	5	1	1						60/60	
4	6	6	1	1							60/60
5	0	4	1	1	12/60	12/60	12/60	12/60	12/60		
6	3	3	2	2				60/60	60/60		
7	5	5	1	1						60/60	
				$C_{0,1,t}$	12/60	12/60	87/60	27/60	27/60	75/60	60/60
				$C_{0,2,t}$	15/60	30/60	30/60	90/60	75/60	0	0
				$C_{1,t}$	12/60	12/60	72/60	12/60	12/60	120/60	60/60
				$C_{2,t}$	0	0	0	120/60	120/60	0	0
				$\Delta C_{1,t}$	0	0	−15/60	−15/60	−15/60	45/60	0
				$\Delta C_{2,t}$	−15/60	−30/60	−30/60	30/60	45/60	0	0

$$
\begin{aligned}
F_{C,\Delta C} &= 2 \cdot \frac{-15 \cdot 15 - 30 \cdot 30 - 30 \cdot 30 + 30 \cdot 90 + 45 \cdot 75}{3600} \\
&\quad + \frac{-15 \cdot 87 - 15 \cdot 27 - 15 \cdot 27 + 45 \cdot 75}{3600} \\
&= \frac{9360}{3600}
\end{aligned}
$$

The minimum was found at cycle 0, so the scheduling of e_7 starts off from the following initial scheduling plan:

i	s_i	l_i	j_i	t_i	$U_{i,0}$	$U_{i,1}$	$U_{i,2}$	$U_{i,3}$	$U_{i,4}$	$U_{i,5}$	$U_{i,6}$
1	2	2	1	1			60/60				
2	3	3	2	2				60/60	60/60		
3	5	5	1	1						60/60	
4	6	6	1	1							60/60
5	0	4	1	1	12/60	12/60	12/60	12/60	12/60		
6	1	1	2	2		60/60	60/60				
7	3	5	1	1				20/60	20/60	20/60	
				$C_{1,t}$	12/60	12/60	87/60	27/60	27/60	75/60	60/60
				$C_{2,t}$	60/60	60/60	0	60/60	60/60	0	0

As e_2 and e_6 are fixed by now, $C_{2,t}$ may not change any more. The steps for e_7 and e_5 are the following:

t	0	1	2	3	4	5	6
$C_{0,1,t}$	12/60	12/60	87/60	27/60	27/60	75/60	60/60

Fixing e_7 to cycle 2:

t	0	1	2	3	4	5	6
$C_{1,t}$	12/60	12/60	132/60	12/60	12/60	60/60	60/60
$\Delta C_{1,t}$	0	0	45/60	$-15/60$	$-15/60$	$-15/60$	0

$$F_{C,\Delta C} = \frac{45 \cdot 87 - 15 \cdot 27 - 15 \cdot 27 - 15 \cdot 75}{3600} = \frac{1980}{3600}$$

Fixing e_7 to cycle 3:

t	0	1	2	3	4	5	6
$C_{1,t}$	12/60	12/60	72/60	72/60	12/60	60/60	60/60
$\Delta C_{1,t}$	0	0	$-15/60$	45/60	$-15/60$	$-15/60$	0

$$F_{C,\Delta C} = \frac{-15 \cdot 87 + 45 \cdot 27 - 15 \cdot 27 - 15 \cdot 75}{3600} = -\frac{1620}{3600}$$

Fixing e_7 to cycle 4:

t	0	1	2	3	4	5	6
$C_{1,t}$	12/60	12/60	72/60	12/60	72/60	60/60	60/60
$\Delta C_{1,t}$	0	0	$-15/60$	$-15/60$	45/60	$-15/60$	0

$$F_{C,\Delta C} = \frac{-15 \cdot 87 - 15 \cdot 27 + 45 \cdot 27 - 15 \cdot 75}{3600} = -\frac{1620}{3600}$$

Note that this plan is equivalent to the previous one as e_7 competes only with e_5 without data dependency, so e_5 introduces a uniform load on the processors in these cycles. In other cycles e_7 increases the number of processors needed above 1, which is a waste of hardware resources.

Fixing e_7 to cycle 5:

t	0	1	2	3	4	5	6
$C_{1,t}$	12/60	12/60	72/60	12/60	12/60	120/60	60/60
$\Delta C_{1,t}$	0	0	$-15/60$	$-15/60$	$-15/60$	45/60	0

$$F_{C,\Delta C} = \frac{-15 \cdot 87 - 15 \cdot 27 - 15 \cdot 27 + 45 \cdot 75}{3600} = \frac{1260}{3600}$$

As a minimum was found for F in cycles 3 and 4, we are free to choose one of them. In this case, due to lack of data dependencies, the choice is irrelevant, so 3 is chosen.

After fixing e_7 to cycle 3, the initial conditions for e_5 are the following:

i	s_i	l_i	j_i	t_i	$U_{i,0}$	$U_{i,1}$	$U_{i,2}$	$U_{i,3}$	$U_{i,4}$	$U_{i,5}$	$U_{i,6}$
1	2	2	1	1			60/60				
2	3	3	2	2				60/60	60/60		
3	5	5	1	1						60/60	
4	6	6	1	1							60/60
5	0	4	1	1	12/60	12/60	12/60	12/60	12/60		
6	0	0	2	2	60/60	60/60					
7	3	3	1	1						60/60	
				$C_{1,t}$	12/60	12/60	72/60	72/60	72/60	12/60	60/60
				$C_{2,t}$	60/60	60/60	0	60/60	60/60	0	0

As we scan the time domain from cycle 0 to 4, e_5 is increasing $C_{1,t}$ either to 60/60 (if fixed to cycles 0, 1 or 4) or to 120/60 (in cycles 2 and 3). The $F_{C,\Delta C}$ values are: 2160/3600 for an operation collision (cycles 2 and 3), where the maximum of $C_{1,t}$ is increased to 120/60; $-1440/3600$ for any other cycle (which sets the maximum of $C_{1,t}$ to 60/60, resulting in a need of one processor for type 1 elements.) Operation e_5 may be fixed to any of these cycles, so cycle 0 (global ASAP cycle) is chosen:

i	s_i	l_i	j_i	t_i	$U_{i,0}$	$U_{i,1}$	$U_{i,2}$	$U_{i,3}$	$U_{i,4}$	$U_{i,5}$	$U_{i,6}$
1	2	2	1	1			60/60				
2	3	3	2	2				60/60	60/60		
3	5	5	1	1						60/60	
4	6	6	1	1							60/60
5	0	4	1	1	12/60	12/60	12/60	12/60	12/60		
6	0	0	2	2	60/60	60/60					
7	3	3	1	1						60/60	
				$C_{1,t}$	12/60	12/60	72/60	72/60	72/60	12/60	60/60
				$C_{2,t}$	60/60	60/60	0	60/60	60/60	0	0

This scheduling plan requires one processor for both types, which is an optimal solution as the system needs four units of type 2 processors ($t_2 + t_6 = 4$) and five units of type 1 processors ($t_1 + t_3 + t_4 + t_5 + t_7 = 5$).

An implementation with one type 1 processor builds the system with $1 \cdot L = 7$ units of type 1 processors, which means two unused units. As only three units of type 2 processors are idle, the solution is optimal.

12.4.2 Pipeline solution based on t_i

The following tables use the data model in [PK89], i.e., processor usage is based on t_i. The extended model, based on q_i, follows in the next section.

During pipelined execution, assuming that $R = 5$,

$$C_{j,0} = W_{j,0} + W_{j,1} \text{ and } C_{j,1} = W_{j,1} + W_{j,6}$$

i	s_i	l_i	j_i	t_i	$U_{i,0}$	$U_{i,1}$	$U_{i,2}$	$U_{i,3}$	$U_{i,4}$	$U_{i,5}$	$U_{i,6}$
1	0	2	1	1	20/60	20/60	20/60				
2	1	3	2	2		20/60	40/60	40/60	20/60		
3	3	5	1	1				20/60	20/60	20/60	
4	4	6	1	1					20/60	20/60	20/60
5	0	4	1	1	12/60	12/60	12/60	12/60	12/60		
6	0	3	2	2	15/60	30/60	30/60	30/60	15/60		
7	2	5	1	1			15/60	15/60	15/60	15/60	
				$W_{1,t}$	32/60	32/60	47/60	47/60	67/60	55/60	20/60
				$W_{2,t}$	15/60	50/60	70/60	70/60	35/60	0	0
				$C_{1,t}$	87/60	52/60	47/60	47/60	67/60		
				$C_{2,t}$	15/60	50/60	70/60	70/60	35/60		

The first operation to be scheduled is e_1.

i	s_i	l_i	j_i	t_i	$U_{i,0}$	$U_{i,1}$	$U_{i,2}$	$U_{i,3}$	$U_{i,4}$	$U_{i,5}$	$U_{i,6}$
1	0	0	1	1	60/60						
2	1	3	2	2		20/60	40/60	40/60	20/60		
3	3	5	1	1				20/60	20/60	20/60	
4	4	6	1	1					20/60	20/60	20/60
5	0	4	1	1	12/60	12/60	12/60	12/60	12/60		
6	0	3	2	2	15/60	30/60	30/60	12/60			
7	2	5	1	1			15/60	15/60	15/60	15/60	
				$W_{1,t}$	72/60	12/60	27/60	47/60	67/60	55/60	20/60
				$W_{2,t}$	15/60	50/60	70/60	70/60	35/60	0	0
				$C_{0,1,t}$	87/60	52/60	47/60	47/60	67/60		
				$C_{0,2,t}$	15/60	50/60	70/60	70/60	35/60		
				$C_{1,t}$	127/60	32/60	27/60	47/60	67/60		
				$C_{2,t}$	15/60	50/60	70/60	70/60	35/60		
				$\Delta C_{1,t}$	40/60	−20/60	−20/60	0	0		
				$\Delta C_{2,t}$	0	0	0	0	0		

$$F_{C,\Delta C} = \frac{40 \cdot 87 - 20 \cdot 52 - 20 \cdot 47}{3600} = \frac{1500}{3600}$$

Starting e_1 at $t = 1$ yields

i	s_i	l_i	j_i	t_i	$U_{i,0}$	$U_{i,1}$	$U_{i,2}$	$U_{i,3}$	$U_{i,4}$	$U_{i,5}$	$U_{i,6}$
1	1	1	1	1		60/60					
2	2	3	2	2			30/60	60/60	30/60		
3	4	5	1	1					30/60	30/60	
4	5	6	1	1						30/60	30/60
5	0	4	1	1	12/60	12/60	12/60	12/60	12/60		
6	0	3	2	2	15/60	30/60	30/60	12/60			
7	2	5	1	1			15/60	15/60	15/60	15/60	
$W_{1,t}$					12/60	72/60	27/60	27/60	57/60	75/60	30/60
$W_{2,t}$					15/60	30/60	60/60	90/60	45/60	0	0
$C_{0,1,t}$					87/60	52/60	47/60	47/60	67/60		
$C_{0,2,t}$					15/60	50/60	70/60	70/60	35/60		
$C_{1,t}$					87/60	102/60	27/60	27/60	57/60		
$C_{2,t}$					15/60	30/60	60/60	90/60	45/60		
$\Delta C_{1,t}$					0	50/60	-20/60	-20/60	-10/60		
$\Delta C_{2,t}$					0	-20/60	-10/60	20/60	10/60		

$$
\begin{aligned}
F_{C,\Delta C} &= \frac{50 \cdot 52 - 20 \cdot 47 - 20 \cdot 47 - 10 \cdot 67}{3600} \\
&\quad + 2 \cdot \frac{-20 \cdot 50 - 10 \cdot 70 + 20 \cdot 70 + 10 \cdot 35}{3600} \\
&= \frac{150}{3600}
\end{aligned}
$$

The next possible starting cycle is $t = 2$.

i	s_i	l_i	j_i	t_i	$U_{i,0}$	$U_{i,1}$	$U_{i,2}$	$U_{i,3}$	$U_{i,4}$	$U_{i,5}$	$U_{i,6}$
1	2	2	1	1			60/60				
2	3	3	2	2				60/60	60/60		
3	5	5	1	1						60/60	
4	6	6	1	1							60/60
5	0	4	1	1	12/60	12/60	12/60	12/60	12/60		
6	0	3	2	2	15/60	30/60	30/60	12/60			
7	2	5	1	1			15/60	15/60	15/60	15/60	
$W_{1,t}$					12/60	12/60	87/60	27/60	27/60	75/60	60/60
$W_{2,t}$					15/60	30/60	30/60	90/60	75/60	0	0
$C_{0,1,t}$					87/60	52/60	47/60	47/60	67/60		
$C_{0,2,t}$					15/60	50/60	70/60	70/60	35/60		
$C_{1,t}$					87/60	72/60	87/60	27/60	27/60		
$C_{2,t}$					15/60	30/60	30/60	90/60	75/60		
$\Delta C_{1,t}$					0	20/60	40/60	-20/60	-40/60		
$\Delta C_{2,t}$					0	-20/60	-40/60	20/60	40/60		

$$F_{C,\Delta C} = \frac{20 \cdot 52 + 40 \cdot 47 - 20 \cdot 47 - 40 \cdot 67}{3600}$$
$$+ 2 \cdot \frac{-20 \cdot 50 - 40 \cdot 70 + 20 \cdot 70 + 40 \cdot 35}{3600}$$
$$= -\frac{2700}{3600}$$

The best result is to fix e_1 to cycle 2. This results in the following initial plan:

i	s_i	l_i	j_i	t_i	$U_{i,0}$	$U_{i,1}$	$U_{i,2}$	$U_{i,3}$	$U_{i,4}$	$U_{i,5}$	$U_{i,6}$
1	2	2	1	1			60/60				
2	3	3	2	2				60/60	60/60		
3	5	5	1	1						60/60	
4	6	6	1	1							60/60
5	0	4	1	1	12/60	12/60	12/60	12/60	12/60		
6	0	3	2	2	15/60	30/60	30/60	12/60			
7	2	5	1	1			15/60	15/60	15/60	15/60	
$W_{1,t}$					12/60	12/60	87/60	27/60	27/60	75/60	60/60
$W_{2,t}$					15/60	30/60	30/60	90/60	75/60	0	0
$C_{1,t}$					87/60	72/60	87/60	27/60	27/60		
$C_{2,t}$					15/60	30/60	30/60	90/60	75/60		

This plan fixes e_2, e_3 and e_4 to their ALAP positions, so the next operation to schedule is e_6. Cycles are scanned from 0 to 3:

i	s_i	l_i	j_i	t_i	$U_{i,0}$	$U_{i,1}$	$U_{i,2}$	$U_{i,3}$	$U_{i,4}$	$U_{i,5}$	$U_{i,6}$
1	2	2	1	1			60/60				
2	3	3	2	2				60/60	60/60		
3	5	5	1	1						60/60	
4	6	6	1	1							60/60
5	0	4	1	1	12/60	12/60	12/60	12/60	12/60		
6	0	0	2	2	60/60	60/60					
7	2	5	1	1			15/60	15/60	15/60	15/60	
$W_{1,t}$					12/60	12/60	87/60	27/60	27/60	75/60	60/60
$W_{2,t}$					60/60	60/60	0	60/60	60/60	0	0
$C_{0,1,t}$					87/60	72/60	87/60	27/60	27/60		
$C_{0,2,t}$					15/60	30/60	30/60	90/60	75/60		
$C_{1,t}$					87/60	72/60	87/60	27/60	27/60		
$C_{2,t}$					60/60	60/60	0	60/60	60/60		
$\Delta C_{1,t}$					0	0	0	0	0		
$\Delta C_{2,t}$					45/60	30/60	−30/60	−30/60	−15/60		

$$F_{C,\Delta C} = 2 \cdot \frac{45 \cdot 15 + 30 \cdot 30 - 30 \cdot 30 - 30 \cdot 90 - 15 \cdot 75}{3600} = -\frac{6300}{3600}$$

i	s_i	l_i	j_i	t_i	$U_{i,0}$	$U_{i,1}$	$U_{i,2}$	$U_{i,3}$	$U_{i,4}$	$U_{i,5}$	$U_{i,6}$
1	2	2	1	1			60/60				
2	3	3	2	2				60/60	60/60		
3	5	5	1	1						60/60	
4	6	6	1	1							60/60
5	0	4	1	1	12/60	12/60	12/60	12/60	12/60		
6	1	1	2	2		60/60	60/60				
7	3	5	1	1				20/60	20/60	20/60	
$W_{1,t}$					12/60	12/60	72/60	32/60	32/60	80/60	60/60
$W_{2,t}$					0	60/60	60/60	60/60	60/60	0	0
$C_{0,1,t}$					87/60	72/60	87/60	27/60	27/60		
$C_{0,2,t}$					15/60	30/60	30/60	90/60	75/60		
$C_{1,t}$					92/60	72/60	72/60	32/60	32/60		
$C_{2,t}$					0	60/60	60/60	60/60	60/60		
$\Delta C_{1,t}$					5/60	0	-15/60	5/60	5/60		
$\Delta C_{2,t}$					-15/60	30/60	30/60	-30/60	-15/60		

$$F_{C,\Delta C} = -\frac{5100}{3600}$$

i	s_i	l_i	j_i	t_i	$U_{i,0}$	$U_{i,1}$	$U_{i,2}$	$U_{i,3}$	$U_{i,4}$	$U_{i,5}$	$U_{i,6}$
1	2	2	1	1			60/60				
2	3	3	2	2				60/60	60/60		
3	5	5	1	1						60/60	
4	6	6	1	1							60/60
5	0	4	1	1	12/60	12/60	12/60	12/60	12/60		
6	2	2	2	2			60/60	60/60			
7	4	5	1	1					30/60	30/60	
$W_{1,t}$					12/60	12/60	72/60	32/60	32/60	80/60	60/60
$W_{2,t}$					0	60/60	60/60	60/60	60/60	0	0
$C_{0,1,t}$					87/60	72/60	87/60	27/60	27/60		
$C_{0,2,t}$					15/60	30/60	30/60	90/60	75/60		
$C_{1,t}$					102/60	72/60	72/60	12/60	42/60		
$C_{2,t}$					0	0	60/60	120/60	60/60		
$\Delta C_{1,t}$					15/60	0	-15/60	-15/60	15/60		
$\Delta C_{2,t}$					-15/60	-30/60	30/60	30/60	-15/60		

$$F_{C,\Delta C} = \frac{2700}{3600}$$

i	s_i	l_i	j_i	t_i	$U_{i,0}$	$U_{i,1}$	$U_{i,2}$	$U_{i,3}$	$U_{i,4}$	$U_{i,5}$	$U_{i,6}$
1	2	2	1	1			60/60				
2	3	3	2	2				60/60	60/60		
3	5	5	1	1						60/60	
4	6	6	1	1							60/60
5	0	4	1	1	12/60	12/60	12/60	12/60	12/60		
6	3	3	2	2				60/60	60/60		
7	5	5	1	1						60/60	
				$W_{1,t}$	12/60	12/60	87/60	27/60	27/60	75/60	60/60
				$W_{2,t}$	60/60	60/60	0	60/60	60/60	0	0
				$C_{0,1,t}$	87/60	72/60	87/60	27/60	27/60		
				$C_{0,2,t}$	15/60	30/60	30/60	90/60	75/60		
				$C_{1,t}$	132/60	72/60	72/60	12/60	12/60		
				$C_{2,t}$	0	0	0	120/60	120/60		
				$\Delta C_{1,t}$	45/60	0	−15/60	−15/60	−15/60		
				$\Delta C_{2,t}$	−15/60	−30/60	30/60	30/60	45/60		

$$F_{C,\Delta C} = \frac{13500}{3600}$$

As e_6 is fixed to cycle 0, the initial plan for scheduling e_7 is

i	s_i	l_i	j_i	t_i	$U_{i,0}$	$U_{i,1}$	$U_{i,2}$	$U_{i,3}$	$U_{i,4}$	$U_{i,5}$	$U_{i,6}$
1	2	2	1	1			60/60				
2	3	3	2	2				60/60	60/60		
3	5	5	1	1						60/60	
4	6	6	1	1							60/60
5	0	4	1	1	12/60	12/60	12/60	12/60	12/60		
6	0	0	2	2	60/60	60/60					
7	2	5	1	1			15/60	15/60	15/60	15/60	
				$W_{1,t}$	12/60	12/60	87/60	27/60	27/60	75/60	60/60
				$W_{2,t}$	60/60	60/60	0	60/60	60/60	0	0
				$C_{0,1,t}$	87/60	72/60	87/60	27/60	27/60		
				$C_{0,2,t}$	60/60	60/60	0	60/60	60/60		

As we have scheduled both type 2 operations, the $F_{C,\Delta C}$ values depend only on the $C_{1,t}$ function. The steps for e_7 are:

t	0	1	2	3	4	5	6
$W_{1,t}$	12/60	12/60	87/60	27/60	27/60	75/60	60/60
$C_{0,1,t}$	87/60	72/60	87/60	27/60	27/60		

Fixing e_7 to cycle 2:

t	0	1	2	3	4	5	6
$W_{1,t}$	12/60	12/60	132/60	12/60	12/60	60/60	60/60
$C_{0,1,t}$	72/60	72/60	132/60	12/60	12/60		
$\Delta C_{1,t}$	−15/60	0	45/60	−15/60	−15/60		

$$F_{C,\Delta C} = \frac{-15\cdot 87 + 45\cdot 87 - 15\cdot 27 - 15\cdot 27}{3600} = \frac{1800}{3600}$$

Fixing e_7 to cycle 3:

t	0	1	2	3	4	5	6
$W_{1,t}$	12/60	12/60	72/60	72/60	12/60	60/60	60/60
$C_{0,1,t}$	72/60	72/60	72/60	72/60	12/60		
$\Delta C_{1,t}$	−15/60	0	−15/60	45/60	−15/60		

$$F_{C,\Delta C} = \frac{-15\cdot 87 - 15\cdot 87 + 45\cdot 27 - 15\cdot 27}{3600} = -\frac{1800}{3600}$$

Fixing e_7 to cycle 4:

t	0	1	2	3	4	5	6
$W_{1,t}$	12/60	12/60	72/60	12/60	72/60	60/60	60/60
$C_{0,1,t}$	72/60	72/60	75/60	12/60	12/60		
$\Delta C_{1,t}$	−15/60	0	−15/60	−15/60	45/60		

$$F_{C,\Delta C} = \frac{-15\cdot 87 - 15\cdot 87 - 15\cdot 27 + 45\cdot 27}{3600} = -\frac{1800}{3600}$$

Note that this plan is equivalent to the previous one as e_7 competes only with e_5 without data dependency, so e_5 introduces a uniform load on the processors in these cycles. In other cycles e_7 increases the number of processors needed above 1, which is a waste of hardware resources.

Fixing e_7 to cycle 5:

t	0	1	2	3	4	5	6
$W_{1,t}$	12/60	12/60	72/60	12/60	72/60	120/60	60/60
$C_{0,1,t}$	132/60	72/60	75/60	12/60	12/60		
$\Delta C_{1,t}$	45/60	0	−15/60	−15/60	−15/60		

$$F_{C,\Delta C} = \frac{45\cdot 87 - 15\cdot 87 - 15\cdot 27 - 15\cdot 27}{3600} = \frac{1800}{3600}$$

As a minimum was found for F in cycles 3 and 4, we are free to choose one of them. In this case, due to lack of data dependencies, the choice is irrelevant, so 3 is chosen.

After fixing e_7 to cycle 3, the initial conditions for e_5 are the following:

i	s_i	l_i	j_i	t_i	$U_{i,0}$	$U_{i,1}$	$U_{i,2}$	$U_{i,3}$	$U_{i,4}$	$U_{i,5}$	$U_{i,6}$
1	2	2	1	1			60/60				
2	3	3	2	2				60/60	60/60		
3	5	5	1	1						60/60	
4	6	6	1	1							60/60
5	0	4	1	1	12/60	12/60	12/60	12/60	12/60		
6	0	0	2	2	60/60	60/60					
7	3	3	1	1				60/60			
$W_{1,t}$					12/60	12/60	72/60	72/60	12/60	60/60	60/60
$W_{2,t}$					60/60	60/60	0	60/60	60/60	0	0
$C_{0,1,t}$					72/60	72/60	72/60	72/60	12/60		
$C_{0,2,t}$					60/60	60/60	0	60/60	60/60		

As e_5 is the last of the operations, it does not cause a problem with data dependencies. As we scan the time domain in increasing order from 0 to 4, all cycles between 0 and $R-1$ are scanned. The scheduling results are as follows
For cycles 0, 1, 2 and 3:

$$F_{C,\Delta C} = \frac{2 \cdot (-12 \cdot 72) + 48 \cdot 72 - 12 \cdot 12}{3600} = \frac{1584}{3600}$$

For cycle 4:

$$F_{C,\Delta C} = \frac{3 \cdot (-12 \cdot 72) + 48 \cdot 12}{3600} = -\frac{2016}{3600}$$

Fixing e_5 to cycle 4 sets the final scheduling plan:

i	s_i	l_i	j_i	t_i	$U_{i,0}$	$U_{i,1}$	$U_{i,2}$	$U_{i,3}$	$U_{i,4}$	$U_{i,5}$	$U_{i,6}$
1	2	2	1	1			60/60				
2	3	3	2	2				60/60	60/60		
3	5	5	1	1						60/60	
4	6	6	1	1							60/60
5	0	4	1	1					60/60		
6	0	0	2	2	60/60	60/60					
7	3	3	1	1				60/60			
$W_{1,t}$					0	0	60/60	60/60	60/60	60/60	60/60
$W_{2,t}$					60/60	60/60	0	60/60	60/60	0	0
$C_{0,1,t}$					60/60	60/60	60/60	60/60	60/60		
$C_{0,2,t}$					60/60	60/60	0	60/60	60/60		

With a latency of 7 and a restart time of 5, this requires one processor of both types (for comparison, pipeline-aware hardware-bound list scheduling produced $L = 9$).

12.4.3 Pipeline solution based on q_i

The following tables document the execution of force-directed scheduling where processor utilization is based on busy time (q_i). As in the previous examples, $R = 5$.

i	s_i	l_i	j_i	t_i	$W_{i,0}$	$W_{i,1}$	$W_{i,2}$	$W_{i,3}$	$W_{i,4}$
1	0	0	1	1	180/180	180/180	60/180		
2	1	3	2	2	60/180	60/180	120/180	180/180	120/180
3	3	5	1	1	120/180	60/180		60/180	120/180
4	4	6	1	1	60/180	60/180			60/180
5	0	4	1	1	72/180	72/180	72/180	72/180	72/180
6	0	3	2	2	90/180	90/180	135/180	135/180	90/180
7	2	5	1	1	90/180	45/180	45/180	90/180	90/180

i	s_i	l_i	j_i	t_i	$W_{i,0}$	$W_{i,1}$	$W_{i,2}$	$W_{i,3}$	$W_{i,4}$
1	1	1	1	1		180/180	180/180	90/180	
2	2	3	2	2	90/180		90/180	180/180	180/180
3	4	5	1	1	180/180	90/180			90/180
4	5	6	1	1	90/180	90/180			
5	0	4	1	1	72/180	72/180	72/180	72/180	72/180
6	0	3	2	2	90/180	90/180	135/180	135/180	90/180
7	2	5	1	1	90/180	45/180	45/180	90/180	90/180

i	s_i	l_i	j_i	t_i	$W_{i,0}$	$W_{i,1}$	$W_{i,2}$	$W_{i,3}$	$W_{i,4}$
1	2	2	1	1			180/180	180/180	180/180
2	3	3	2	2	180/180			180/180	180/180
3	5	5	1	1	180/180	180/180			
4	6	6	1	1		180/180			
5	0	4	1	1	72/180	72/180	72/180	72/180	72/180
6	0	3	2	2	90/180	90/180	135/180	135/180	90/180
7	2	5	1	1	90/180	45/180	45/180	90/180	90/180

Fixing to cycle 1.

i	s_i	l_i	j_i	t_i	$W_{i,0}$	$W_{i,1}$	$W_{i,2}$	$W_{i,3}$	$W_{i,4}$
1	1	1	1	1		180/180	180/180	180/180	
2	2	2	2	2			180/180	180/180	180/180
3	4	5	1	1	180/180	90/180			90/180
4	5	6	1	1	90/180	90/180			
5	0	4	1	1	72/180	72/180	72/180	72/180	72/180
6	0	3	2	2	90/180	90/180	135/180	135/180	90/180
7	2	5	1	1	90/180	45/180	45/180	90/180	90/180

i	s_i	l_i	j_i	t_i	$W_{i,0}$	$W_{i,1}$	$W_{i,2}$	$W_{i,3}$	$W_{i,4}$
1	1	1	1	1		180/180	180/180		
2	3	3	2	2	180/180			180/180	180/180
3	5	5	1	1	180/180	180/180			
4	6	6	1	1		180/180			
5	0	4	1	1	72/180	72/180	72/180	72/180	72/180
6	0	3	2	2	90/180	90/180	135/180	135/180	90/180
7	2	5	1	1	90/180	45/180	45/180	90/180	90/180

Fixing to cycle 3.

i	s_i	l_i	j_i	t_i	$W_{i,0}$	$W_{i,1}$	$W_{i,2}$	$W_{i,3}$	$W_{i,4}$
1	1	1	1	1		180/180	180/180		
2	3	3	2	2	180/180			180/180	180/180
3	5	5	1	1	180/180	180/180			
4	6	6	1	1		180/180			
5	0	0	1	1	180/180	180/180			
6	0	3	2	2	90/180	90/180	135/180	135/180	90/180
7	2	5	1	1	90/180	45/180	45/180	90/180	90/180

i	s_i	l_i	j_i	t_i	$W_{i,0}$	$W_{i,1}$	$W_{i,2}$	$W_{i,3}$	$W_{i,4}$
1	1	1	1	1		180/180	180/180		
2	3	3	2	2	180/180			180/180	180/180
3	5	5	1	1	180/180	180/180			
4	6	6	1	1		180/180			
5	1	1	1	1		180/180	180/180		
6	0	3	2	2	90/180	90/180	135/180	135/180	90/180
7	2	5	1	1	90/180	45/180	45/180	90/180	90/180

i	s_i	l_i	j_i	t_i	$W_{i,0}$	$W_{i,1}$	$W_{i,2}$	$W_{i,3}$	$W_{i,4}$
1	1	1	1	1		180/180	180/180		
2	3	3	2	2	180/180			180/180	180/180
3	5	5	1	1	180/180	180/180			
4	6	6	1	1		180/180			
5	2	2	1	1			180/180	180/180	
6	0	3	2	2	90/180	90/180	135/180	135/180	90/180
7	2	5	1	1	90/180	45/180	45/180	90/180	90/180

i	s_i	l_i	j_i	t_i	$W_{i,0}$	$W_{i,1}$	$W_{i,2}$	$W_{i,3}$	$W_{i,4}$
1	1	1	1	1		180/180	180/180		
2	3	3	2	2	180/180			180/180	180/180
3	5	5	1	1	180/180	180/180			
4	6	6	1	1		180/180			
5	3	3	1	1				180/180	180/180
6	0	3	2	2	90/180	90/180	135/180	135/180	90/180
7	2	5	1	1	90/180	45/180	45/180	90/180	90/180

i	s_i	l_i	j_i	t_i	$W_{i,0}$	$W_{i,1}$	$W_{i,2}$	$W_{i,3}$	$W_{i,4}$
1	1	1	1	1		180/180	180/180		
2	3	3	2	2	180/180			180/180	180/180
3	5	5	1	1	180/180	180/180			
4	6	6	1	1		180/180			
5	4	4	1	1	180/180				180/180
6	0	3	2	2	90/180	90/180	135/180	135/180	90/180
7	2	5	1	1	90/180	45/180	45/180	90/180	90/180

Fixing to cycle 3.

i	s_i	l_i	j_i	t_i	$W_{i,0}$	$W_{i,1}$	$W_{i,2}$	$W_{i,3}$	$W_{i,4}$
1	1	1	1	1		180/180	180/180		
2	3	3	2	2	180/180			180/180	180/180
3	5	5	1	1	180/180	180/180			
4	6	6	1	1		180/180			
5	3	3	1	1				180/180	180/180
6	0	0	2	2	180/180	180/180	180/180		
7	2	5	1	1	90/180	45/180	45/180	90/180	90/180

i	s_i	l_i	j_i	t_i	$W_{i,0}$	$W_{i,1}$	$W_{i,2}$	$W_{i,3}$	$W_{i,4}$
1	1	1	1	1		180/180	180/180		
2	3	3	2	2	180/180			180/180	180/180
3	5	5	1	1	180/180	180/180			
4	6	6	1	1		180/180			
5	3	3	1	1				180/180	180/180
6	1	1	2	2		180/180	180/180	180/180	
7	3	5	1	1	120/180	60/180		60/180	120/180

i	s_i	l_i	j_i	t_i	$W_{i,0}$	$W_{i,1}$	$W_{i,2}$	$W_{i,3}$	$W_{i,4}$
1	1	1	1	1		180/180	180/180		
2	3	3	2	2	180/180			180/180	180/180
3	5	5	1	1	180/180	180/180			
4	6	6	1	1		180/180			
5	3	3	1	1				180/180	180/180
6	2	2	2	2			180/180	180/180	180/180
7	4	5	1	1	180/180	90/180			90/180

i	s_i	l_i	j_i	t_i	$W_{i,0}$	$W_{i,1}$	$W_{i,2}$	$W_{i,3}$	$W_{i,4}$
1	1	1	1	1		180/180	180/180		
2	3	3	2	2	180/180			180/180	180/180
3	5	5	1	1	180/180	180/180			
4	6	6	1	1		180/180			
5	3	3	1	1				180/180	180/180
6	3	3	2	2	180/180			180/180	180/180
7	5	5	1	1	180/180	180/180			

Fixing to cycle 0.

i	s_i	l_i	j_i	t_i	$W_{i,0}$	$W_{i,1}$	$W_{i,2}$	$W_{i,3}$	$W_{i,4}$
1	1	1	1	1		180/180	180/180		
2	3	3	2	2	180/180			180/180	180/180
3	5	5	1	1	180/180	180/180			
4	6	6	1	1		180/180			
5	3	3	1	1				180/180	180/180
6	0	0	2	2	180/180	180/180	180/180		
7	2	2	1	1			180/180	180/180	

i	s_i	l_i	j_i	t_i	$W_{i,0}$	$W_{i,1}$	$W_{i,2}$	$W_{i,3}$	$W_{i,4}$
1	1	1	1	1		180/180	180/180		
2	3	3	2	2	180/180			180/180	180/180
3	5	5	1	1	180/180	180/180			
4	6	6	1	1		180/180			
5	3	3	1	1				180/180	180/180
6	0	0	2	2	180/180	180/180	180/180		
7	3	3	1	1				180/180	180/180

i	s_i	l_i	j_i	t_i	$W_{i,0}$	$W_{i,1}$	$W_{i,2}$	$W_{i,3}$	$W_{i,4}$
1	1	1	1	1		180/180	180/180		
2	3	3	2	2	180/180			180/180	180/180
3	5	5	1	1	180/180	180/180			
4	6	6	1	1		180/180			
5	3	3	1	1				180/180	180/180
6	0	0	2	2	180/180	180/180	180/180		
7	4	4	1	1	180/180				180/180

i	s_i	l_i	j_i	t_i	$W_{i,0}$	$W_{i,1}$	$W_{i,2}$	$W_{i,3}$	$W_{i,4}$
1	1	1	1	1		180/180	180/180		
2	3	3	2	2	180/180			180/180	180/180
3	5	5	1	1	180/180	180/180			
4	6	6	1	1		180/180			
5	3	3	1	1				180/180	180/180
6	0	0	2	2	180/180	180/180	180/180		
7	5	5	1	1	180/180	180/180			

Fixing to cycle 2.

13

The design tool PIPE

PIPE was developed at the Department of Control Engineering and Informatics (formerly Department of Process Control), Technical University of Budapest, as an educational software tool for designing pipeline data flow devices.

PIPE processes an elementary operations graph (EOG) where the nodes of the graph denote elementary operations and the edges their direct data dependencies. Given a predefined restarting period, *PIPE*—if necessary— inserts buffers to meet this period. *PIPE* schedules EOGs with the assumptions described in Chapter 3, using an extended version of force-directed scheduling to optimize resource usage.

PIPE generates different variations of the graph by moving synchronization buffers. For every variation allocation is performed: elementary operations which are not working concurrently may be combined into one unit. *PIPE* tries to find these units.

The software itself is written in Perl and runs under several variations of UNIX. It has been tested extensively under several versions of Linux and Sun Solaris, and runs on Windows-based machines as well. (For Windows-based execution, a Perl environment, such as produced by the Cygwin or ActiveState Perl, is required.) The performance penalty of using a (partially) interpreted language is compensated for by portability. The main *PIPE* modules are listed in Table 1.

The following documentation in this chapter documents the development version of *PIPE* as of 25 September 2000. This version may be copied from the CD-ROM. For an up-to-date copy of *PIPE*, the following URL is recommended:

```
http://www.iit.bme.hu/~pipe/
```

For historical reasons, the current *PIPE* version carries the name *PIPE2*. It is the first major rewrite of the software. It is distributed under a free software licence.

13.1   Usage

The *PIPE* system is a set of independent modules, each optimized for a given task. *PIPE* itself provides a wrapper around the collection of modules. Command-line arguments are processed by the wrapper and passed to the corresponding modules.

Table 1   Main *PIPE* modules

rmloop	Open recursive loops.
type2time	Map operation type to timing.
restart	Execute algorithm RESTART.
topology	Generate.
asapalap	Find ASAP and ALAP timing.
sched.fce	Force-directed scheduling of the EOG.
synchronize	Insert synchronization buffers, where necessary.
alloc	Allocate graph using a greedy heuristic.
controlflow	Extract control flow from schedule.

The general format of the invocation of the *PIPE* program follows UNIX traditions:

```
pipe  [{-l|-r|-rr} value]  [-v [-v ...]]  [-b]  [input files...]
```

The *PIPE* invocation follows Table 2 which summarizes command-line switches.

The last parameter is the name of the input file. If no input is given, *PIPE* reads its standard input (as in traditional UNIX usage).

To aid running extended benchmarks in *PIPE*, a wrapper exists around the *PIPE* framework. The p2scan module (*PIPE* II scan) iterates a time value, such as restart time or latency, across an interval. This scanning mode of execution is useful if a cost versus time tradeoff is sought.

Table 2   *PIPE* command-line switches

Switch	Explanation
-l	Prescribe system latency. By default, *PIPE* assumes the system targets minimum latency. Latency may be absolute or relative. In the latter case, a value of '+N' prescribes a latency N cycles more than the possible minimum.
-r	Prescribe restart time (R). By default, *PIPE* assumes the system operates in non-pipelined mode, i.e., $L = R$.
-rr	Prescribe execution restart time (R). Used if scheduling targets a different restart time than the actual execution restart time.
-v	Verbose mode. May be repeated for more detail. The *PIPE* modules document the verbosity level required for each detail.

13.2   Input

PIPE uses a simple hardware description language as input. This declares functional elements and gives the interconnection between them.

Input graphs are described by direct dependencies between elementary operations and elementary operation types. The first input stages expand type information to timing, which is processed by later stages.

As an example, a multiplier ('m1') is directly connected to the adder 'a1', which processes a direct system input ('IN'). The system input obviously has no predecessors.

```
IN       SYSTEM
a1       add     IN
m1       mul     a1
```

System parameters are described in structured comments. As an example, the above operations are supplemented by the following timing information:

```
#       type    mult    4
#       type    SYSTEM  0
```

13.3   Output

PIPE's output contains the result of allocation: which functional elements are combined into one. The properties of elementary operations change in two important aspects:

1. Scheduling fixes the starting time of operations, therefore, no freedom remains in the time domain.

2. Elementary operations are assigned to physical processors during allocation.

The output description is otherwise practically identical to the input format.

Having read Chapters from 11 to 13, solving the benchmark problems (Section 16.3) by using the CAD tool PIPE *is advised.*

14

Effective graph generation

The transformation between a problem description and a data dependency graph is a step which results in a significant reduction of freedom during high-level synthesis. It is possible to improve the quality of the hardware structure if a suitable graph generation method is used during the generation of the EOG. High-level synthesis usually takes its input in some form of an artificial language, i.e., VHDL or one of several similar languages [Dew97]. These descriptions take the form of functions which must be transformed to a hardware realization using the steps of initial allocation, scheduling and allocation.

Problems that are given as functions may be transformed to data dependency graphs which feature operations as nodes in the graph and direct data transfers as branches. The structure (or layout) of this graph affects the efficiency of scheduling since it sets the intervals in which an operation may be moved (*operation time frame*) [AV98]. The length of the time frame of an operation is equal to the (operation) mobility. Operations with a higher mobility may usually be scheduled yielding better results, since they possess a higher degree of freedom. Note that layout is used as a description of graph structure and not in the sense which is usual in high-level synthesis (i.e., that of silicon structures).

It is usually better to postpone the limitations to the stage of scheduling. Otherwise the scheduling step may not influence the overall efficiency of the system since the scheduler gets the graph in a fixed state (without mobility). Since scheduling methods affect the graph by inserting buffers to the branches, original operations are usually referred to as functional operations (as opposed to buffer operations). Buffers are inserted into the graph to increase the data propagation time of a given branch (and to provide storage between slow operations) and are generally referred to as delay.

The properties of the graph are described using two numeric values:

depth refers to the number of levels a graph has, i.e., the maximum number of sequentially executed functional operations. A graph with a greater depth requires more time to calculate its output values (i.e., has a higher latency).

width describes the maximum number of simultaneously executing operations in a graph. It is useful to use width both as a time function and as a parameter of the whole graph. As a time function, the width belonging to cycle t ($W_{j,t}$) is equal to the number of type j functional operations executing in that cycle. As a global parameter, W_j must be an upper bound to $W_{j,t}$ values:

$$W_j = \max_{0 \leq t < R} W_{j,t}$$

To build a system with a width of W_j, one must build a sufficient number of type j processors so that there are always enough processors to execute all operations scheduled to a given cycle. Therefore, the number of processors (M_j) and graph width (W_j) are related as follows:

$$\max_{0 \leq t < R} W_{j,t} = W_j \leq M_j \quad \text{for every processor type}$$

For our investigations we take a simple function that evaluates the sum

$$S = a + b + c + d + e + f + g + h$$

This function is special since its operations are commutative and the operations work on data of identical type. This function is not a very special case since FIR filters have the same core structure [Kun82] (see Figure 54 for a comparable FIR layout, where the adders show a possible implementation of the above sum). The only important difference is that this simplified model does not contain multiple operation types.

As an example, by using a function

$$f_k = w_k \cdot x_k$$

an eight FIR filter may be described as the following:

$$S_k = f_k + f_{k-1} + f_{k-2} + f_{k-3} + f_{k-4} + f_{k-5} + f_{k-6} + f_{k-7}$$

With the same data model, an eight order convolution has the same S function (and, therefore, the same EOG) if the f function is defined as

$$f_k = w_k \cdot x_{7-k}$$

assuming one numbers samples starting at 0.

The number of functional operations in the graph is denoted by $N-1$, which means that this problem type requires N operands. An elementary operation requires T cycles to produce its output after its inputs are stable.

14.1 Binary structures

One of the possible extreme structures of the graphs belonging to this function is the binary structure, composed in such a way that data propagates in a binary tree (Figure 48). Since two is the maximum of data inputs for an operation, the binary structure is the global optimum if depth is to be optimized. Since a binary tree with N data inputs ($N \geq 2$) has

$$V = \lceil \log_2 N \rceil$$

levels, the latency of the graph may not be lower than $V \cdot T$.

The width of a binary layout is equal to 2^V. The number of required processors is decreasing as data enters deeper levels of the graph since two operations supply the inputs of every operation in the graph. This results in an increasing number of unused processors as time increases.

Another possible name of this structure is *triangular layout*.

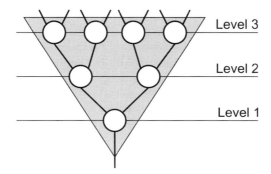

Figure 48   Binary structure (triangular layout)

Obviously processor utilization is an exponentially decreasing function of time and so it has its maximum during the first T cycles of execution. Should the binary structure be described using brackets, the graph presented in Figure 48 is equivalent to the following organization:

$$S = ((a + b) + (c + d)) + ((e + f) + (g + h))$$

14.2   Linear structures

Another extreme structure type is the linear structure, where functional operations form a linear branch (Figure 49). Since no pair of operations executes simultaneously, this organization offers more chance for allocation than a binary layout.

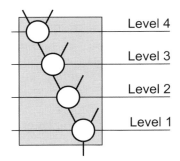

Figure 49   Linear structure (rectangular layout)

The width of a linear structure is uniform. Since this structure requires fewer processors than a binary layout, it is generally cheaper. The disadvantage of the linear graph is the increased latency: as N operations must execute in a linear (sequential) way, the result may not appear before $N \cdot T$ cycles after the system input appears. Should buffers be inserted into the system, total latency would be increased proportionally to the number of levels.

Should buffers be inserted into the graph, the most probable way is to insert a buffer between adjacent functional operations, since their busy times are all equal (as they are connected in such a way that their busy time is equal to $2 \cdot T$). This increases the linear latency (LL) to

$$LL = N \cdot T + (N - 1),$$

The latency of a binary structure under similar conditions is extended to

$$LB = T \cdot V + (V - 1) = T \cdot \lceil \log_2 N \rceil + (\lceil \log_2 N \rceil - 1)$$

as the decreased depth reduces the number of direct connections between functional operations.

A linear graph structure is equivalent to the following bracket pairs:

$$S = (((((((a + b) + c) + d) + e) + f) + g) + h)$$

14.3   Transitions between binary and linear structures

Should a binary structure be scheduled using an algorithm capable of dealing with a hardware constraint, the resulting structure is an extended version of the binary triangle (an intermediate structure). As an extreme value, a maximum of one may be prescribed for graph width, which is equivalent to the requirement of the linear structure. The result of this scheduling is equivalent to the linear layout if we consider the width of the graph and the number of utilized buffers (Figure 50). Since the binary structure may be extended to an equivalent of the linear structure, it is a useful starting point for feasibility calculations. Considering the maximal hardware requirements of a binary layout, a balance must be maintained between latency and graph width.

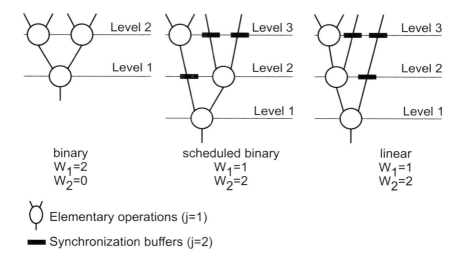

Figure 50   Transition between a binary and a linear structure

14.4   Fixed-width binary structures

A useful method to improve the properties of the binary layout is to order the operations in a binary tree with an additional condition for the maximum of the simultaneously used processors. This structure may be produced by an algorithm similar to list scheduling (with a hardware constraint).

The example given in Figure 51 started off as a binary layout. Since a maximum width of 3 was prescribed for the system, some of the operations (marked with a star) were moved so that the number of simultaneously utilized processors was kept below 4. This step required the operations to be separated from their successors, which is indicated with the delay elements.

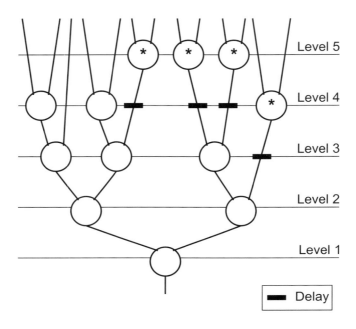

Figure 51   Binary structure produced under a width limit

Three methods are available for the generation of this structure. The first method generates the binary tree starting from the root (the last element), delaying any operations which would violate the hardware limit.

Another possible method is to generate a full binary tree and decimate the operations starting from the operations which are nearest to the system inputs (leaves of the tree). The third algorithm to generate a fixed-width binary structure is to proceed with the generation of the binary tree up to the point where the width is equal to the width limit. Linear structures may be appended to these points so that the width is not increased further.

14.5 Capacity calculation for intermediate structures

A fixed-width binary structure may be generated in the following way:

1. Generate the necessary number of binary levels. These levels are completely filled with operations except for the last one (the one with the highest number of operations) which may be incomplete (i.e., with some operations missing). The condition to achieve this is

$$2^{A-2} < W \leq 2^{A-1}$$

where A is the number of binary levels and W is the desired graph width. The conditions imply that the binary tree is deep enough, so that it has a suitable number of operations at its last level and it is not deeper than needed (i.e., the number of operations on the second lowest level is less than W).

In Figure 52(a), a partial binary graph is generated for $W = 3$ (which implies $A = 3$).

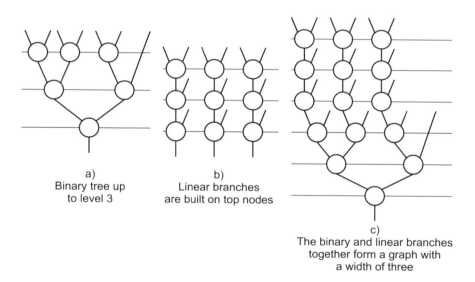

a)
Binary tree up
to level 3

b)
Linear branches
are built on top nodes

c)
The binary and linear branches
together form a graph with
a width of three

Figure 52 Generating a fixed-width binary tree

2. The last binary level consists of W operations. The remaining $2^{A-1} - W$ positions on this level are not filled with functional operations; these connections are used as direct system inputs. This organization offers a

total of $2 \cdot W + 2^{A-1} - W$ data inputs since the W nodes have two inputs each, while the rest of the connections are single (see Figure 53(a)).

Should linear branches be appended to the suitable nodes, one of the data inputs would be occupied. Since the number of suitable nodes is W, the number of data inputs of such an extended binary structure is 2^{A-1} as the previous value is decreased by W.

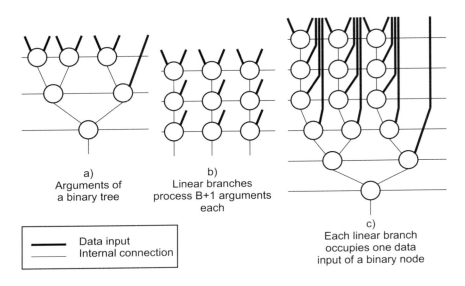

a)
Arguments of
a binary tree

b)
Linear branches
process B+1 arguments
each

c)
Each linear branch
occupies one data
input of a binary node

Data input
Internal connection

Figure 53   System data inputs in a fixed-width binary tree

3. Linear branches are appended to the operations of the last level of the binary structure, where one input of these operations is connected to the output of the linear branch, the other being a system input. A linear structure with B levels calculates the result of B operations, and so takes $B + 1$ system inputs.

   The depth of the linear branches must be chosen so that the minimum and maximum values do not differ by more than one. This results in the lowest overall latency as there is no way to implement the same structure with fewer levels. To find B, one must solve the following inequality (after finding A based on W):

   $$W \cdot (B + 1) + 2^{A-1} \geq N$$

   The first term counts the number of linear system inputs, the second one the data inputs of the last level of the binary structure. See Figure 53.

The inequality prescribes that the number of direct data inputs is sufficient to process all N inputs.

This B is the maximum of the linear depth values. It is also possible to add linear branches with a lower number of operations $(B - 1)$. The number of these branches is found to be $W \cdot (B + 1) + 2^{A-1} - N$ since this decrease guarantees that the structure offers a total of N data inputs.

Figure 53 is a graph where $W = 3$, $A = 3$ (implied) and $B = 3$ (exactly). The system resembles a FIR filter of order 16 ($N = 16$).

14.6 Restrictions

The method outlined in this chapter is useful only in systems where the operations are commutative. This is the case, however, with most of the filters, which are high-level synthesis targets, both in benchmarks and in applications. The operations may be non-elementary, for example a FIR filter features two operations (a product and a sum) in each of the nodes. It is therefore feasible to schedule the internals after finding a suitable layout. As an example, the digital convolution (eight-order version) may be implemented so that it has the necessary delay at its inputs, see Figure 54. The second part of the graph is then suitable for generation with this method, since its graph is then similar to the FIR algorithm in structure.

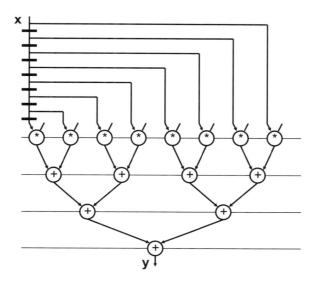

Figure 54   A possible layout of an eight-order digital convolution

The functional operations are the same as in the FIR filter, since they consist of *multiply-add* pairs. In this case, an optimizable layout was generated after applying intuition. There are no known graph-generation algorithms which may be used in a general case.

Having read this chapter, solving Problem 11 (Chapter 16) is advised.

15

System-level synthesis principles

Due to technological development, the complexity of systems to be designed and the components to be used is increasing. Complex systems may consist of both hardware and software components. These two kinds of components influence each other, and have complementary advantages. Combining advantageous hardware and software properties in a common design procedure is the main motivation of *hardware-software codesign* (HSCD). HSCD consists of a proper decomposition into hardware and software, and design, simulation, and testing of such systems.

The selection of the architecture in HSCD is traditionally based on intuition and designer experience. Therefore, the probability of design errors is high, and design and manufacturing time may be relatively long. Intuitive steps may result in non-optimal utilization of components. HSCD simulation and testing are difficult to execute step by step without some systematic design methodology. Computer-aided methods called *system-level synthesis* (SLS) solve these problems at the system level by considering global properties instead of local (bottom-up) optimization.

CAD tools capable of system-level synthesis contain HLS algorithms. Most SLS approaches are based on the use of formal models to describe the behaviour of the system at a sufficiently high level of abstraction. Decisions on the decomposition into hardware and software *contexts* are made at the formal model level. System decomposition is usually based on prior designs by using existing and tested components. These components are complex units offered by the vendors, often as standard and adaptable products. Due to the complexity of such components, they are called *intellectual property* (IP) units. The adaptability of IPs is based on some kind of flexibility or reprogrammability. Therefore, the same types of IP may be applied many times for similar or identical tasks in a system. This influences the decomposition and sets the goal of reusing IPs. Obviously, reusability and flexibility are strongly related and reuse in design, testing, and manufacturing is beneficial since it decreases time-to-market.

Based on the above considerations, one of the main goals of SLS is to decompose the system with as much IP reuse as possible. Obviously, coordination and proper control of the applied IPs and the information exchange between them are also important tasks. Most standard IPs are accessible through standardized communication protocols. HLS methods may be applied in SLS not only in IP generation, but also in designing the interfaces between IPs. HLS steps may be used in the realization of communication protocols between different execution contexts (ECs).

Very important features of the SLS CAD tools are simulation, test, and rapid prototyping facilities. Some tools perform synthesis by assuming a target structure fixed in advance. In such cases, the hardware and software IP components may be modelled and described by different high-level languages, depending on which is most suitable for each of them. Certain tools solve even the co-simulation in different languages and therefore do not need conversion between hardware and software description languages.

Using a set of predefined, well-known target structures, the design process of a *mixed-context environment* (MCE) system may be finished faster than an iterative design process [ABIC⁺98, AJ97].

Other SLS procedures explore different distributions of operations in different design domains. In a simple hardware-software system, two environments are available for the placement of elementary operations (software and hardware). HSCD systems balance the advantages of differences in *execution contexts* to maximize system performance. *Execution contexts* are the largest possible subsystems in the target environment where direct communication is possible between components in the same context. Communication is direct if it may be realized using entirely combinatorial logic.

To enable reuse of HLS heuristics in an MCE, the MCE system should be described as an extension of generally accepted HLS models. Such an extended description may be used to simulate, optimize, and synthesize MCE systems with well-known HLS technologies and tools. Mapping multiple-context system specifications to an entirely HLS-compatible system description enables immediate reuse of purely hardware or software-based (*single-context*) optimization and synthesis tools. Such a system description may be called *Multiple-Context High-Level Synthesis* (MCHLS).

Software implementations are assumed to be executed on off-the-shelf, general-purpose processors. Application-specific, synthesized processors [Pag94] are not covered in this text. (Application-specific processor solutions, such as described in [Pag95b], do not necessarily feature multiple execution contexts.)

15.1   Partitioning

In an MCE system, selecting an efficient combination of hardware and
software subsystems is a special case of the *partitioning problem* [Knu95].
Partitioning assigns subsystems to hardware and software environments,
creating "software" and "hardware" partitions of the set of blocks. In MCHLS,
the partition cost function is based entirely on the cost of edges in the partition
cut. Some partitioning heuristics, such as those developed in supercomputing,
target "balanced" partitions, i.e., partitions with a small difference between
the number of nodes between partitions. These balanced partitioners solve an
entirely different problem, and are applicable in MCHLS. Similarly, HSCD
partition costs are not directly related to system geometry, and geometry-
based partitioning techniques (such as used in VLSI layout design [AL98],
[Las93]).

Finding the partitions with the minimum cost in a system is,
unfortunately, NP-complete [Hoc97] [GJ79]. As the partitioning problem
is not tractable, several heuristic approximations have emerged. Literature
differentiates between *global* (*construction*) and *local* (*improvement*)
algorithms. Construction algorithms generate a partition based on global
performance metrics, and are usually applied in a non-iterative fashion.
Improvement algorithms use an already existing partition and attempt to
enhance system properties by applying incremental changes to it.

15.1.1   Construction algorithms

For some MCHLS systems, especially for smaller graphs, initial partitions
provided by straightforward, greedy algorithms are sufficient. Greedy
algorithms search the large partition solution space without lookahead,
guaranteeing termination. Starting from one of the extreme system
configurations (i.e., purely software or hardware), the system is iteratively
refined until it meets cost constraints. The steps to get a good initial partition
depend on the primary constraint of the system, i.e., the dominant member of
the cost function. In time-constrained systems, a solution with more hardware
is generally better; similarly, in a system with space or cost constraints, an
entirely software solution may be a better starting point. Because of the
difference between these conditions, the initial partition is generated using
slightly different methods:

- In systems under dominant cost constraints,

    1. Generate an initial, extreme system configuration: assign all operations
       to software. An entirely software solution is assumed to be the cheapest.

2. Terminate if system meets timing requirements, or is "sufficiently close". (The acceptance range is, obviously, system-dependent.)

3. Transform the critical path or critical paths to hardware. Find the new critical path.

4. Repeat from 2.

• In systems under dominant time constraints,

1. Generate an initial, extreme system configuration: assign all operations to hardware. Pure hardware is the fastest, most expensive solution.

2. Terminate if system meets cost requirements.

3. Transform operations outside the critical path to software (in time cycles with the highest hardware load).

4. Repeat from 2.

In practical terms, the applied heuristic is an expanded version of the greedy set covering the heuristic [Hoc97], but the choice of operation to be moved (i.e., coloured) is better suited to the MCHLS design process. Also, the system may be expanded to handle more than two execution contexts, an advantage not present in the original form of greedy graph growing.

15.1.2   Improvement algorithms

Local partitioning algorithms, as refinements of existing partitions, try to select efficient local changes that improve quality. A number of efficient local algorithms are derivatives of the *Kernighan-Lin algorithm* [KL70].

The Kernighan-Lin algorithm swaps pairs of operations in an existing partition in an iterative way. The algorithm selects the operation pairs based on a local cost function and attempts to optimize the overall change in the global cost function. System cost function is defined as a non-decreasing function of the *cut size* of the partition, i.e., the number of edges connecting operations in different execution contexts. The cost change caused by moving an operation across an execution context boundary is described by a *difference function* in each partition. The Kernighan-Lin algorithm selects operations as candidates for swapping based on their difference function, attempting to move operations with maximal differences. Operations that had been moved in a given improvement pass may not be moved any more in the same pass (they are said to be *locked*). Locking prevents oscillation.

With $\mathcal{O}(n^2)$ time complexity (and a convenient, small constant factor), the Kernighan-Lin algorithm is reasonable to use in small to medium graphs (up to several thousands of operations). An important extension to the Kernighan-Lin algorithm has been created by Fiduccia and Mattheyses [FM82]. This modified version executes in $\mathcal{O}(n)$ or $\mathcal{O}(m \log n)$ time and moves individual operations without attempting the swapping of operation pairs. Graph operations are scanned sequentially, evaluating system cost after attempting to relocate each of the operations to a different partition. Each such move (i.e., an operation and its target partition) is checked for final system cost. The move with the lowest final system will be selected as the local optimum.

Each pass of the Kernighan-Lin algorithm and the Kernighan-Lin-Fiduccia-Mattheyses algorithm continues as long as there are available unlocked operations. After the pass is over, the total cost change is evaluated, and the next pass is attempted only if the previous one improved system cost.

For an efficient estimation of system cost in HSCD, the Kernighan-Lin algorithm must be extended with weights and performance attributes to properly model the effect of multiple-context communications. Since execution context switches should not affect data values, just representation, delay is a suitable model of the context switch. The actual length of context switch delay is a function of bit width, source context and destination context. Such a cost function may be constructed based on the timings of the hardware-software connections, communication protocols, and the properties of processor interfaces.

15.2   Clustering

In some hardware-software codesign environments, graph transformations are applied to the system description before partitioning to reduce the size of the solution space. By inhibiting the partitioning process from separating certain elementary operations, solution times decrease considerably with no performance loss. Since no context switch may take place inside such groups of operations ("clusters"), the number of possible partitions is decreased.

Even if the problem formulation may be similar to partitioning, this process is part of the design for a slightly different reason than the partitioning problem. Unlike partitioning, where global metrics are important, local grouping serves a different purpose, reduction of partitioning solution space. This additional partitioning step therefore has a separate name, *clustering*. For established hardware-software codesign environments, where a large database of standard modules is available, an efficient way of clustering is the identification of operation groups that could be easily implemented in an already existing module. In top-down designs, higher-level blocks may be used as a basis of clusters.

15.2.1   Software allocation

Software compilation differs from pure hardware HLS in the placement
of scheduling and allocation. Software instruction scheduling and register
allocation are usually performed in the same phase, as opposed to hardware
designs, where allocation generally happens after scheduling. A possible reason
is that inserting an additional register to compensate for over-utilization is
possible in hardware. In software, one may emulate more registers than are
physically available by code transformations. Saving to and restoring register
values from system memory is referred to as using *spill code* [ASU88]. Since
spill code alters the data path, feedback is required in the design process.
The performance penalty of spill code (i.e., additional load-store pairs), is
considerable, especially in RISC systems.

A possible approach to integrate scheduling and allocation is presented
in [NP98]. By splitting scheduling in two (global and local rounds) and
performing allocation between two different schedulers, the second scheduler
pass may compensate for the effect of any spill code introduced by the
allocator.

Several variants of list scheduling offer extensions to handle strict resource
limits. The solution to such problems is to reorganize the data-flow to a given
concurrency by delaying some of the operations. A typical implementation
of this greedy algorithm proceeds with a list scheduler under resource
constraints. The allocator then simply scans the time cycles in increasing
order, and assigns execution units sequentially. Since the schedule complies
with resource constraints, there may be no conflict in allocation. Under these
conditions, the allocator has to select the best execution unit to implement
each operation.

As a disadvantage of resource-constrained schedulers, latency of the design
is out of designer control. In practical systems, scheduling is performed under
a resource constraint, and the constraint is relaxed until the latency becomes
satisfactory. In software systems, spill code may be inserted after this step, if
the number of required execution units exceeds that of the available ones.

15.3   Multiple-Context High-Level Synthesis

This section introduces the process model and the heuristics that were found
useful in SLS-oriented extensions of the HLS problem. Assuming familiarity
with the steps of HLS, compilation, clustering, and partitioning, the section
presents the necessary changes between a single-environment and a MCHLS
process.

The MCHLS extensions over single-context designs are not limited to
environments with two execution contexts (binary partitions), and the results

are applicable to systems with more than two execution contexts.

Since the *Multiple-Context High-Level Synthesis* (MCHLS) design process is assumed to be a transparent extension of *High-Level Synthesis* (HLS), the inputs and outputs of the MCHLS design are mainly the same as the traditional HLS process. The only observable difference is in the output, since MCHLS terminates with a register-transfer level description of hardware subsystems and a data-flow graph for software modules; the latter is obviously not present in HLS results (Figure 55). The high-level description input of both HLS and MCHLS is assumed to be a flow-graph, which in turn is usually generated from a description at an even higher level of abstraction.

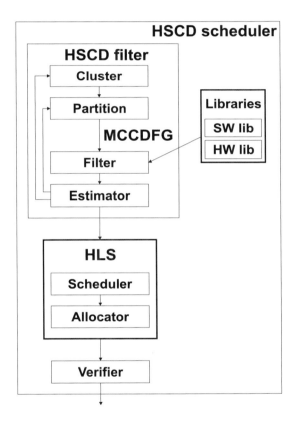

Figure 55 Partitioning as a filter for HLS

Since it is desirable to reuse as much of the existing results as possible, a modular framework is beneficial to the SLS process. Extensive research has been conducted for efficient heuristics for clustering, partitioning, scheduling, and allocation. By implementing these steps as separate modules, the freedom of selecting different heuristics or approximation algorithm for a given task is possible. Since scheduling and allocation stages of SLS may be realized in an integrated way, a feasible solution is to implement the clustering and partitioning stages as layers around the existing scheduling and allocation libraries (Figure 55). The clustering and partition stages simply supply input to an "external" component for scheduling and allocation. By separating different models, the task of debugging and simulation also becomes easier, since different representations of the problem become available at the boundaries between different steps of the design process. (Generating observable results during the design process may be conveniently reused during simulations and testing [Ros98].)

Since the most popular scheduling and allocation packages are usually incapable of dealing with the complications of multiple-context environment systems, the design framework transforms multiple-context environment data-flow graphs to single-context environment descriptions. It is the responsibility of the partitioning algorithm to hide the hardware-software boundary details from the scheduling and allocation stages. Since the MCHLS process describes the EOG with context-switch information as well, data reduction is required after the partitioning stage. A step is inserted after partitioning to annotate the data-flow graph with context switch operations. A suitable name for this step is *context mapping*, since it transforms abstract extended elementary operations (EEOs) ("FFT in software") to fixed numbers based on the available technology and libraries ("FFT in t_i cycles (in x_i context)") (Figure 55). Context mapping also inserts context-switch operations to model the communications on data transfers across execution context boundaries.

The input of context mapping is the *multiple-context EOG (MCEOG)*, and the output is an expanded form of the EOG. The output is an EOG, which may be separated to execution contexts. The EOG sections in different execution contexts may be processed directly by the scheduling and allocation stage and the code generator (Figure 55). Note that the compilation steps of software include instruction scheduling and allocation, but are treated as part of the compilation process, and not discussed in detail.

The scheduling and allocation phase of both software generation and hardware synthesis returns an intermediate representation. The output of software generation is source code for a state-machine description realizing the functions of the data-flow graph passed to it. This raw source code lacks further optimization, and relies on the efficiency of the target compiler environment for performance improvements. For specific systems, the code generator may be extended by knowledge of the underlying compiler to generate more efficient structures.

The output format of hardware synthesis is usually *register-transfer level* information. Since most HLS design environments feature elaborate, stand-alone RTL synthesizers, RTL synthesis may be treated as a black box system, and no special consideration is made to optimize the RTL description.

15.4   Transfer model of multiple-context environments

In order to accommodate a mixed hardware-software context environment (*multiple-context environment*, MCE), one must be able to represent execution context in addition to the elementary operations of the EOG. Two trivial possibilities are:

1. attach an execution attribute to each operation,

2. label edges with context switch information.

In the latter case the destination and source contexts are encoded as an attribute of the edge (i.e., the data transfer) and context information is not represented in operations (elementary operations). A combination of the two methods is chosen, as representation changes from edge attributes to operation attributes after the partitioning phase.

In the beginning, by storing the execution environment as an operation attribute, one increases the information content of the system EOG without increasing the number of operations. As partitioning assigns elementary operations to execution contexts, changing an operation attribute is easier since topological EOG properties (such as the number of operations or edge information) do not change with each step.

After partitioning, context switches should be merged into the EOG so that scheduling and allocation do not have to deal with properties of the EOG data transfers. (Most popular scheduling algorithms are unable to deal with connection information if it is represented in EOG edges instead of operations.) After such a transformation, the EOG describes the context switch as a property of a fictitious elementary operation. A suitable method of transforming context switches to operations is to insert a "transfer" operation to the system.

Transfer operations encode the context switch information of each context-switch edge in an operation without changing data in any way. These transfers are practically delays corresponding to the cost of crossing context boundaries, and should be treated as delays in every other respect. (Additional side effects, such as byte-order reordering or synchronization on context boundaries, are assumed to occur inside the operation, without affecting the data itself. If there is a requirement for non-trivial data transformations, they are better represented as a functional operation in addition to the context switch.)

Since context-switch operations are inserted only where a data transfer crosses the boundary between two execution contexts, the increase of operation numbers is moderate. (Especially since a good partition minimizes the cost of cuts, which is related to the number of edges crossing partition boundaries.)

Even if each additional operation increases later optimization times, changing the representation model of context switches improves efficiency for a number of reasons:

1. All information is stored in operations after graph generation. Data transfers (the edges of the EOG) do not contain any additional information other than direct dependencies.

   Since the final structure representation relies on a single kind of data, implementation becomes easier. The only data structure a scheduler has to deal with is a set of operations, with connections serving no other purpose than describing direct data dependencies. This is the native operation model of most scheduling and allocation heuristics.

2. As no new information is obtained on the data transfer after relocating "edge information" to "operation information", the properties of the transfer operations need not be changed after partitioning.

   Since operation properties are fixed before scheduling and allocation steps, the EOG may be optimized with algorithms that are able to handle constant execution times only. Most of the heuristic, polynomial complexity algorithms offer good scheduling and allocation properties only if operation execution times are fixed for each elementary operation before scheduling.

   The properties that are available at the time of transformation include bit width (n), start (s) and destination (d) execution context. Based on this information, the execution time and complexity requirement of the data transfer may be expressed as

   $$t(n, s, d)$$

   and

   $$c(n, s, d),$$

   respectively. The $t(\cdot)$ and $c(\cdot)$ functions are based on heuristic results or optimization targets as well as hardware architecture and interfaces. Both $t(\cdot)$ and $c(\cdot)$ functions are expected to be available at the start of the HLS process, and are supplied as technology libraries to the MCHLS environment.

The time and cost functions are usually highly non-linear in nature as functions of bit width or execution environments. Intel microprocessors, where 8-bit transfers may take the same amount as 32-bit transfers, are good examples of such non-linear behaviour. Misaligned (i.e., loaded from non-word-aligned memory addresses), heavily penalized RISC memory accesses are also typical in this sense. As an example, a PowerPC 403GC (a RISC microprocessor widely used in embedded applications) suffers a slowdown of up to several hundred times with misaligned data since hardware hides the misaligned access by throwing an expensive exception on every misaligned memory access.

By using transfer time as the single important attribute of context switches, the amount of information is reduced to a feasible level. As implementation details of the transfer implementation are not required until the stage of interface generation, disregarding all non-time-related attributes of context switches does not discard important information [JRV+98]. The interface synthesis at the end of the synthesis process generates the software and hardware for implementing the transmission protocol.

15.4.1   Multiple-context data-flow graphs

The EOG of purely hardware-oriented HLS offers a simple, effective way of modelling elementary operations. To address the different optimization criteria of HSCD, changes must be made to the elementary operation model of HLS, since a MCE requires additional properties to describe HSCD-specific features. Additional properties may be difficult to handle in later steps of the design process, as already existing scheduling and allocation functions are usually unable to use this information.

To keep HSCD problems at a manageable size, initial performance estimation and optimization has to stop at a relatively high level of abstraction so that the number of blocks to optimize (*problem size*) stays low. This is possible if problem decomposition does not expand the complete problem hierarchy in the beginning, or if clustering reduces EEO count considerably. At a high level of abstraction, "elementary" operations are no longer truly elementary by HLS definitions, since they are not executing exactly one elementary operation in the data path. This contradicts with a basic assumption of high-level synthesis since elements of the initial data-flow graph are supposedly truly elementary in a traditional HLS process.

Composite operations are operations realized by internal decomposition to several elementary operations.

In most practical hardware-software codesign systems, EOG operations are not truly elementary operations during partitioning. MCE operations in the multiple-context environment EOG are usually composite. Dealing with composite operations is definitely an advantage in partitioning, but may inhibit efficient scheduling and allocation (top-down design makes low-level optimization more difficult). To increase scheduling and allocation performance, the internals of the operations should be expanded before scheduling.

As an example of elementary and extended elementary operations, consider a popular DSP application, *GSM speech processing*. GSM cellular phones feature a sophisticated model of speech compression with finite state machines providing correction to the reconstructed data stream. The block diagram of the prediction unit (*GSM Regular Pulse Excitation – Long Term Prediction (RPE/LTP) encoder*) comprises 19 blocks [Pin96]. Such a low number of blocks is useful for partitioning purposes (Figure 56). None of these blocks are primitive in the HLS sense, since they feature decoders, quantizers, and basic filters. (In fact, several of the blocks are used as standalone benchmarks for HLS. Two examples are the inverse filter (e_9) and the weighting filter (e_{13}).)

For ease of discussion, composite operations are called "extended elementary operations", regardless of their actual implementation. Similarly, the EOG of composite operations is referred to as the *extended elementary operation graph* (EEOG) to differentiate between truly elementary and composite operations. Elementary operation attributes are listed in Table 3.

In addition to the properties of elementary operations in HLS, the following attributes have to be represented in the EEOG:

Execution context, x_i, denotes the environment of e_i. This attribute is assigned during partitioning. After context mapping, the execution context attribute is not referenced directly, since all operations will be defined in terms of timing and resource usage. In the following example, operations mapped to hardware have $x_i = 1$ while software execution is denoted by $x_i = 2$.

Table 3   Elementary operation attributes in MCHLS

Property	Notation	Assigned during
Start time	b_i	scheduling
Execution time	t_i	context mapping
Operation type	j_i	context mapping
ASAP start time	s_i	scheduling
ALAP start time	l_i	scheduling
Execution context	x_i	partitioning
Operation category	k_i	graph generation

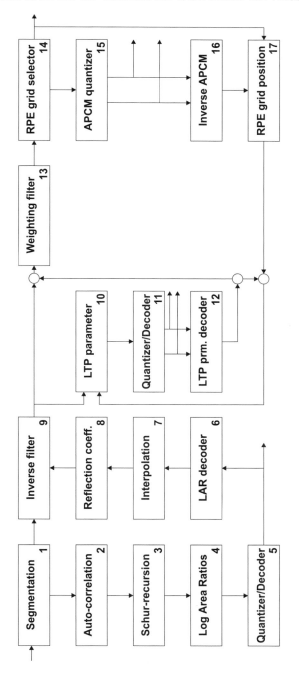

Figure 56   Block diagram of GSM example

Operation complexity, n_i, is the significant data size of the input data of e_i. This attribute may be important where it influences implementation costs or operation timing. A typical measure of n_i is the bit width of input values, but other measures of complexity are possible.

Operation category, k_i, is similar to operation type j_i, but it is an initial property of the elementary operation. An example operation category could be "Fast Fourier Transform (FFT)" without reference to implementation. Initial operation type depends only on the elementary operation itself and has no connection to the execution context of the given operation. Operation category is used only during partitioning and context mapping, where operation category and execution context are combined to generate the operation type of the elementary operation. To represent the differences between software and hardware implementations, one must reconsider the properties of operation type as well.

Operation type, j_i, in multiple-context environments includes execution context. As an example, a software Fast Fourier Transform (FFT) operation is different from a hardware implementation for modelling purposes, and the operation types of e_i (a "software FFT" operation) and e_j (a "hardware FFT" operation) are different, even if both are FFT implementations (i.e., $k_i = k_j$).

Operation type in multiple-context environments may be determined after the partitioning step, and is done during context mapping. For each operation of the data-flow graph, the context mapping assigns operation type as a function of operation execution context and operation category:

$$j_i = j_i(k_i, x_i)$$

For accurate calculations, the operation type may include operation complexity as well. This is the case, for example, if the underlying hardware modules are generated from different models based on complexity.

Operation type is used during scheduling and allocation. Assigning different operation types to elementary operations of the same category and different execution contexts speeds up allocation. Using the operation type as an allocation attribute (i.e., if $j_k = j_l$, e_k may compete with e_l for system resources), the number of concurrence constraints in the system is decreased. Thus, even if $k_5 = k_{15}$ (both e_5 and e_{15} use "quantizer" resources), the allocator heuristic need not set up a constraint on the concurrence of e_5 and e_{15}, as $x_5 \neq x_{15}$. In other words, even if the busy times of e_5 and e_{15} overlap, there is no resource violation problem since e_5 (mapped to software) ties up a CPU resource, while e_{15} occupies a piece of ASIC circuitry in the same cycles.

15.5 Multiple-context HLS design process

As an example, a stripped-down version of a practical system is used. The block diagram in Figure 56 on page 161 is a section of a GSM speech coder circuitry [Pin96]. This part of the GSM DSP application is often used as an example of practical HSCD systems. The example is only a section of the GSM coder since the whole system would be too large for effective demonstration in the text. (Certain submodules of limited functionality, such as adders and shifters, have been removed from the original block diagram to increase readability.)

The example graph is a fixed-point Linear Predictive Coder (LPC) where 160 13-bit resolution sound samples are compressed to 260-bit encoded blocks. The algorithm calculates an estimated time signal based on previous sound samples, and passes on the difference between estimated sequence and actual samples. The graph contains 17 EEOGs with an additional, low-complexity operation, e_{18}. The blocks in Figure 56 are treated as extended elementary operations at the partitioning phase (i.e., no clustering takes place). See Figure 57 on page 165.

The original attributes of the GSM example are given in Table 4.

The steps taken during iterative rounds may be executed in the following way:

1. Partition the graph into execution contexts, i.e., assign x_i.

2. Insert context-switch operations to the system by replacing edges crossing execution context boundaries. Timing of context-switch operations depends on destination and source contexts, bit width, and communication protocol. This information is supplied by the context mapping technology files.

3. Expand the internals of extended elementary operations. Generate the necessary elementary operation graphs and merge them by replacing each with their subsystems' graphs.

4. Assign operation types to elementary operations based on category and execution context:

$$j_i = j_i(k_i, x_i)$$

The sample system, with the partition shown in Figure 58 on page 168, has the final operation types shown in Table 5. The extended elementary operation attributes after context mapping are shown in Table 6.

5. Assign execution times:

$$t_i = t_i(j_i, n_i)$$

6. Insert transfer operations:

$$t_k = t_k(x_i, x_j, n_j)$$

7. Start scheduling and allocation.

The output is an execution plan of the design, prescribing an estimated schedule of data and control transfers.

Table 4   Extended elementary operation attributes of GSM example

i	k_i	k_i (symbolic)	**Name in GSM block diagram**
1	1	segm	Segmentation
2	2	filter	Auto-correlation
3	3	schur	Schur-recursion
4	4	param	LAR calculation
5	5	quant	Quantizer/coder
6	6	decoder	LAR decoder
7	7	interp	Interpolation
8	8	coeff	Reflection coefficients
9	2	filter	Inverse filter
10	4	param	LTP parameter
11	5	quant	Quantizer/coder
12	6	decoder	LTP parameter decoder
13	2	filter	Weighting filter
14	9	grid	RPE grid selection
15	5	quant	APCM quantizer
16	5	quant	Inverse quantizer
17	9	grid	RPE grid positioning
18	10	adder	Adder

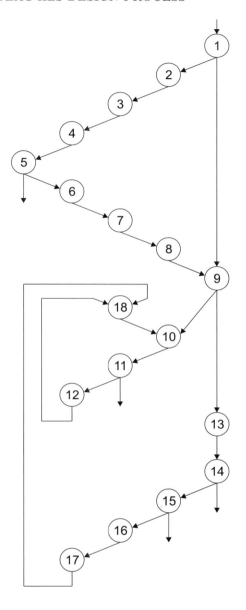

Figure 57 Extended elementary operation graph of GSM example

Table 5   Extended elementary operation attributes of partitioned
GSM example

i	k_i		x_i		j_i	
	#	symbolic	#	symbolic	#	symbolic
1	1	segm	1	hardware	1	hardware segmentation
2	2	filter	1	hardware	2	hardware filter
3	3	schur	2	software	3	software Schur
4	4	param	2	software	4	software parameter
5	5	quant	2	software	5	software quantizer
6	6	decoder	2	software	6	software decoder
7	7	interp	2	software	7	software interpolation
8	8	coeff	1	hardware	8	hardware coefficients
9	2	filter	1	hardware	2	hardware filter
10	4	param	2	software	4	software parameter
11	5	quant	2	software	5	software quantizer
12	6	decoder	2	software	6	software decoder
13	2	filter	1	hardware	2	hardware filter
14	9	grid	1	hardware	9	hardware grid
15	5	quant	1	hardware	10	hardware quantizer
16	5	quant	1	hardware	10	hardware quantizer
17	9	grid	2	software	11	software grid
18	10	adder	2	software	12	software adder

Table 6 Extended elementary operation attributes of partitioned
GSM example after context mapping

i	k_i	k_i (symbolic)	Name in GSM block diagram
1	1	segm	Segmentation
2	2	filter	Auto-correlation
3	3	schur	Schur-recursion
4	4	param	LAR calculation
5	5	quant	Quantizer/coder
6	6	decoder	LAR decoder
7	7	interp	Interpolation
8	8	coeff	Reflection coefficients
9	2	filter	Inverse filter
10	4	param	LTP parameter
11	5	quant	Quantizer/coder
12	6	decoder	LTP parameter decoder
13	2	filter	Weighting filter
14	9	grid	RPE grid selection
15	5	quant	APCM quantizer
16	5	quant	Inverse quantizer
17	9	grid	RPE grid positioning
18	10	adder	Adder
19	5	cswitch	Context switch
20	5	cswitch	Context switch
21	9	cswitch	Context switch
22	10	cswitch	Context switch

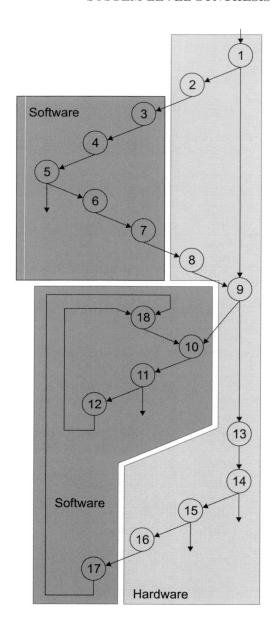

Figure 58   Extended elementary operation graph of partitioned
GSM example

16

Solved problems

16.1 Problems

Problem 1

The elementary operation graph (EOG) in Figure 59 consists of the operations as follows:

e_3, e_4:	SUBTRACTION,	$t_3 = t_4 = 10$
e_7, e_8:	ADDITION,	$t_7 = t_8 = 10$
e_6:	DIVISION,	$t_6 = 40$
e_1, e_2, e_5:	MULTIPLICATION,	$t_1 = t_2 = t_5 = 30$

1. Determine the shortest pipeline restarting period allowed for the EOG without any modification on it.

2. Reduce the shortest restarting period by inserting the minimal number of buffers only. How many additional clock cycles should be added to the original latency in this case?

3. Reduce the shortest restarting period by inserting the minimal number of buffers and by applying as few multiple copies of operations as possible. Synchronize the EOG and determine the ASAP schedule. How many additional clock cycles should be added to the original latency in this case?

4. Calculate the mobility of each elementary operation in the EOG modified according to Problem 1.3.

5. How could the restarting period $R = 12$ be achieved?

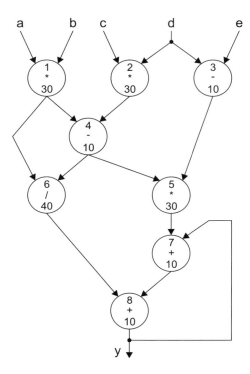

Figure 59   EOG for Problem 1

Problem 2

The elementary operation graph (EOG) in Figure 60 consists of the operations as follows:

e_3	SUBTRACTION,	$t_3 = 10$
e_2, e_5, e_6	ADDITION,	$t_2 = t_5 = t_6 = 10$
e_4	DIVISION,	$t_4 = 40$
e_1	MULTIPLICATION,	$t_1 = 30$

1. Modify the EOG for achieving the pipeline restarting period $R = 7$ by inserting the minimal number of buffers and by applying as few multiple copies of operations as possible. Synchronize the EOG and determine the ALAP schedule. How many additional clock cycles should be added to the original latency?

2. Does each addition operation need a separate adder, if the required restarting period is $R = 42$?

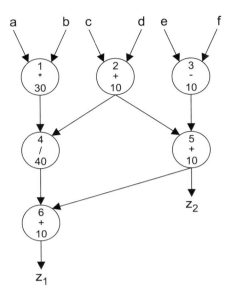

Figure 60   EOG for Problem 2

Problem 3

Let a datapath be constructed for calculating the following recursive algebraic expression:

$$z = \frac{\dfrac{a}{b} \cdot z_{-1} + b + c}{c + d}$$

where a, b, c, d are the input variables, z denotes the actual result and z_{-1} stands for the result obtained at the previous restart.

1. Draw a proper EOG consisting of the following elementary operations with at most two inputs:

ADDITION,	$t = 1$
DIVISION,	$t = 6$
MULTIPLICATION,	$t = 2$

2. Modify the EOG for achieving the shortest possible pipeline restarting period by inserting the minimal number of buffers and by applying as few multiple copies of operations as possible. Calculate the mobility of each operation.

3. Calculate the shortest restarting period which enables the allocation of all addition operations to a single common adder.

Problem 4

The frequency f_n of a photon starting from the surface of the sun is measured as a frequency f_r at a distance r. Based on the measurement, f_n can be calculated as follows:

$$f_n = f_r \cdot \frac{r - a}{r},$$

where a is a constant value.

1. Draw a proper EOG consisting of the following elementary operations with at most two inputs:

SUBTRACTION,	$t = 5$
DIVISION,	$t = 40$
MULTIPLICATION,	$t = 30$

   Try to minimize the value of synchronizing delay effects in constructing the EOG.

2. Determine the shortest restarting period, which is achievable by inserting the minimal number of buffers only. Calculate the minimal values of delay effects for synchronizing the modified EOG.

3. Assuming that the clock frequency of the datapath modified according to Problem 4.2 is 10 MHz, calculate the maximal error in sensing f_r compared with the continuous measurement, if the changing rate of f_r is not greater than 0.1 Hz/s.

Problem 5

According to the Doppler principle, the frequency f_o of a voice source moving with a speed v_f can be calculated from the frequency f measured at the place of the sensor moving with a speed v_e as follows:

$$f_o = f \cdot \frac{c - v_f}{c + v_e},$$

where c denotes the speed of light.

1. Draw a proper EOG consisting of the following elementary operations
   with at most two inputs:

SUBTRACTION,	$t = 5$
ADDITION,	$t = 5$
DIVISION,	$t = 40$
MULTIPLICATION,	$t = 30$

Try to minimize the value of synchronizing delay effects in constructing
the EOG.

2. Determine the shortest restarting period, which is achievable by
   inserting the minimal number of buffers only. Calculate the minimal
   values of delay effects for synchronizing the modified EOG.

3. Determine a schedule for the EOG of Problem 5.2, which enables
   the operations ADDITION and SUBTRACTION to be allocated to a
   common functional unit.

4. How much time would be allowed (i.e. how fast would instruments
   need to be) for measuring f, v_e and v_f if the datapath had to start
   an interaction within 0.02 ms after a change of f_0 (real-time mode)?

5. Does the restarting period calculated in Problem 5.2 remain valid, if the
   instruments with the measuring speed required for the real-time mode
   according to Problem 5.4 are applied at the input of the datapath?
   If not, then how could this restarting period be preserved in spite of
   assuming that no faster instruments are at one's disposal?

Problem 6

Assuming $R = 6$ as the desired restarting period, insert the necessary buffers
into the non-synchronous transfer sequence in Figure 61.

Problem 7

Assuming $R = 5$ as the desired restarting period, insert the necessary buffers
into the non-synchronous transfer sequence in Figure 62.

Problem 8

Assuming $R = 4$ as the desired restarting period, insert the necessary buffers
into the non-synchronous transfer sequence in Figure 63.

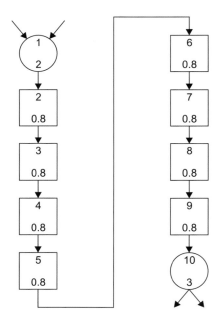

Figure 61   Transfer sequence for Problem 6

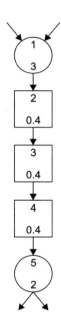

Figure 62   Transfer sequence for Problem 7

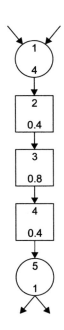

Figure 63   Transfer sequence for Problem 8

Problem 9

Assuming $R = 5$ as the desired restarting period, insert the necessary buffers into the non-synchronous transfer sequence in Figure 64.

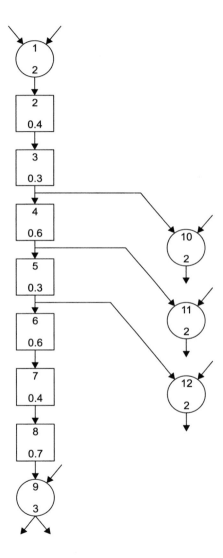

Figure 64   Transfer sequence for Problem 9

Problem 10

Given the following approximation of a part of a differential equation system, find the resource requirements for an implementation serving two processes simultaneously. The implementation is based on the EOG in Figure 65 (without enumerating constants in the EOG).

$$\Delta y = \Delta t \cdot \min \left(k_1, k_2 x + \frac{k_3 y}{k_4 y + k_5} \right)$$

Assume that a multiplication takes 16 cycles, a division requires 24 cycles, the minimum operation terminates in 2 cycles and an addition requires 4 cycles. There is a loop latency limit of 140 cycles. The restart time is $R = 40$.

Enumerate the start times of processors implementing the solution.

Problem 11

Generate an EOG for the 128th order FIR filter structure described by the following equation:

$$y_j = \sum_{k=1}^{128} w_k x_{j-k}$$

Assume that a 'multiply-and-add' elementary operation primitive is available. This elementary operation has three inputs, one each for sample (x), coefficient and additive term. The execution time of the multiply-add pair is 16 cycles.

Find the solution with the lowest latency in non-pipelined execution if the maximum of concurrently executing multiply-and-add pairs may not be more than 18.

Find the latency of the generated system if the restart time is 22.

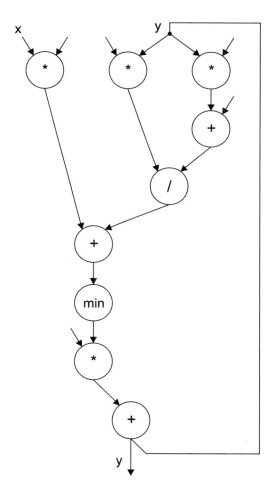

Figure 65 An example of recursive execution

16.2 Solutions

Solution 1

1. Without any modification: $\min R = 71$, because the maximal value of busy times is $q_1 = 70$ (Figure 66(a)).

2. By inserting buffers only, $\min R = 42$ can be achieved, because the maximal value of busy times is reduced to $q_6 = 41$ (Figure 66(b)). The three inserted buffers prolong the latency by 2 clock cycles, since they influence the longest transfer sequence.

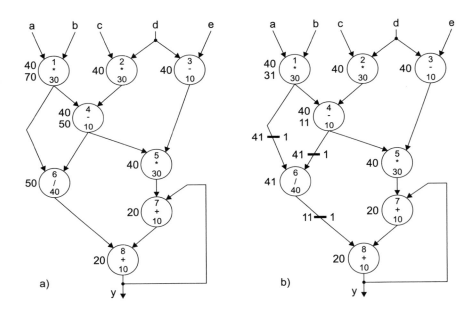

Figure 66 Illustration of the solution of Problems 1.1 and 1.2

3. The solution can be obtained by applying algorithm RESTART for the shortest restarting period. The loop with duration time $T = 20$ limits the shortest restarting period to $\min R = 21$. To achieve this value, multiple copies cannot be avoided for e_1, e_2, e_5 and e_6:

$$c_1 = c_2 = c_5 = \left\lceil \frac{30 + 2}{21} \right\rceil = 2$$

$$c_6 = \left\lceil \frac{40 + 2}{21} \right\rceil = 2$$

The multiple operations require additional buffers at the inputs of e_1, e_2, e_5 (Figure 67(a)), but there is no need for additional buffers at their outputs, because $10 < 2 \cdot 21 - 30$. For similar reasons, the replication of e_5 also does not require output buffer; and e_6 is already followed by a buffer inserted in earlier steps. Synchronizing problems may arise at the inputs of e_5, e_6 and e_8. According to algorithm SYNC:

$$z_{5,3} = \max p_{5,3} = 42 - 11 = 31$$
$$\min p_{5,3} = 31 + 30 + 1 - 2 \cdot 21 = 20$$

$$z_{6,1} = \max p_{6,1} = 42 - 32 = 10$$
$$\min p_{6,1} = 10 + 40 + 1 - 2 \cdot 21 = 9$$

$$z_{8,7} = \max p_{8,7} = 83 - 82 = 1$$
$$\min p_{8,7} = 1 + 10 + 10 - 21 = 0$$

The modifications made by RESTART cause one additional clock cycle in latency compared with Figure 66(b) following from the buffers at the inputs of e_2.

4. By moving upwards each maximal delay effect belonging to the ASAP schedule, the situation illustrated in Figure 67(b) can be obtained, from which no further upwards moving is possible. Thus, this is the ALAP schedule. Non-zero mobility domains belong to operations e_3 and e_5 only:

$$mob_3 = b_3^{ALAP} - b_3^{ASAP} = 32 - 0 = 32$$
$$mob_5 = b_5^{ALAP} - b_5^{ASAP} = 43 - 42 = 1$$

5. The expression represented by the EOG in Figure 59 is

$$y = \frac{a \cdot b - c \cdot d}{a \cdot b} + (a \cdot b - c \cdot d) \cdot (d - e) + y^{-1},$$

where y^{-1} denotes the result obtained at the previous restart. Obviously, the order of the additions e_7 and e_8 can be inverted as shown in Figure 68. Thus, the duration time of the loop is $T = 11$ instead of 20. Therefore, the reduced loop limits $\min R$ to 12 instead of 21. (Without the buffer in the feedback, the assumptions for EOG would be violated.)

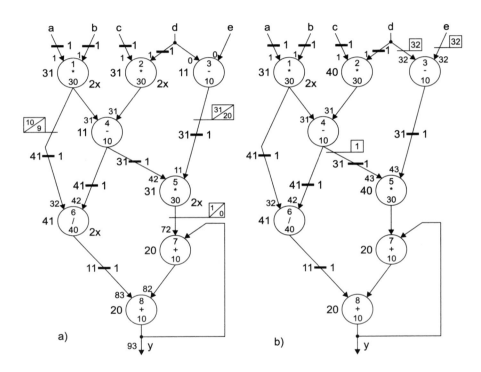

Figure 67   Illustration of the solution of Problems 1.3 and 1.4

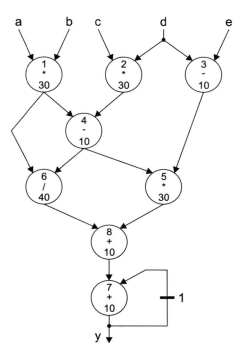

Figure 68   Illustration of the solution of Problem 1.5

Solution 2

1. By applying algorithm RESTART for the desired restarting period $R = 7$, no buffer insertion is performed and all operations should be replicated as shown in Figure 69(a). The calculations for the numbers of copies are as follows:

$$c_1 = \left\lceil \frac{30+2}{7} \right\rceil = 5$$

$$c_2 = c_3 = c_5 = c_6 = \left\lceil \frac{10+2}{7} \right\rceil = 2$$

$$c_4 = \left\lceil \frac{40+2}{7} \right\rceil = 6$$

For calculating the ALAP schedule, the values of the $z_{i,h}$s as the maximal synchronizing delay effects should be calculated. Algorithm

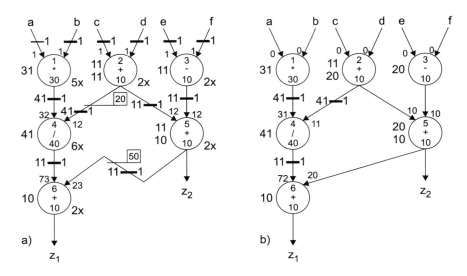

Figure 69 Illustration of the solution of Problem 2.1

SYNC provides these values placed according to the ASAP schedule as shown in Figure 69(a). In this case, moving the delay effects upwards is not possible without prolonging the latency, so the ASAP and ALAP schedules are identical. In other words, each operation has zero mobility.

The buffers inserted in the longest transfer sequence (e_1, e_4, e_6) cause three additional clock cycles. This is the prolongation of latency.

2. In Figure 69(b), the EOG is shown which is obtained by applying RESTART for $R = 42$. There are no inserted buffers after the additions and no multiple copies are needed in this case. Obviously, the additions e_2, e_5 and e_5, e_6 are concurrent pairs, since the busy times of direct successors are overlapping according to the assumptions made for EOG. Therefore, the non-concurrence of the pair e_2, e_6 is to be checked only. Applying algorithm CONCHECK, the inequalities

$$q_2 + q_6 < R$$
$$b_6 - b_2 > q_2$$

should hold for non-concurrence. Replacing the pessimistic values from Figure 69(b) yields:

$$20 + 10 < 42$$
$$72 - 0 > 20$$

Thus, the non-concurrence is not excluded. For the final conclusion, the inequality

$$\frac{b_i - b_j + q_i}{R} < Int\left(\frac{b_i - b_j - q_j}{R}\right)$$

has to be checked. Replacing the values

$$\frac{0 - 72 + 20}{42} < Int\left(\frac{0 - 72 - 10}{42}\right), \quad \text{i.e.} \quad -1.238 < -1$$

is obtained. Thus, e_2 and e_6 are non-concurrent if $R = 42$, i.e. they do not need separate adders.

Solution 3

1. The expression should be rearranged in order to form the shortest loop:

$$z = \frac{a}{b \cdot (c + d)} \cdot z_{-1} + \frac{b + c}{c + d}$$

The EOG is shown in Figure 70.

2. The duration of the loop is $T = 2 + 1 = 3$, so the restarting period cannot be shorter than 4.

   Applying algorithm RESTART, buffer insertions are obtained at the outputs of e_3 only as shown in Figure 71. No additional buffers are required at the outputs of multiple operations e_4, e_5. Note that all of the other buffers serve as input buffers of multiple operations e_4, e_5:

$$c_4 = c_5 = \left\lceil \frac{6 + 2}{4} \right\rceil = 2$$

   To obtain the ASAP schedule, the maximal synchronizing delay effects are to be determined. These values in Figure 71 are 1, 3 and 4. The delays 1 and 3 cannot be moved upwards according the relocation rules. Thus, the operations in transfer sequence e_1, e_3, e_5, e_6, e_7 have zero mobility. Delay 4 is movable upwards as far as the dotted frames, so e_2 and e_4 have non-zero mobility:

$$mob_2 = 4 - 0 = 4$$
$$mob_4 = 6 - 2 = 4$$

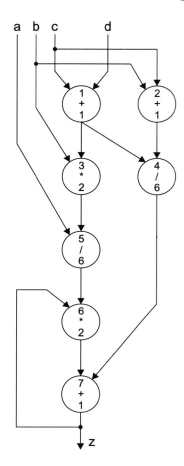

Figure 70   Illustration of the solution of Problem 3.1

3. For each pair from the three addition operations, the concurrence is to be checked as a function of the restarting period. Either algorithm CONCHECK or inequality (7.2) in Chapter 7 can be used for this aim. The calculation is easier if inequality (7.2) is chosen in this case.

   Let the pair e_1, e_7 be checked at first, because both operations have zero mobility:

   $$\frac{0 - 12 - 3}{R} \leq K \leq \frac{0 - 12 + 3}{R}$$

   The smallest R excluding the integer solution is 8.

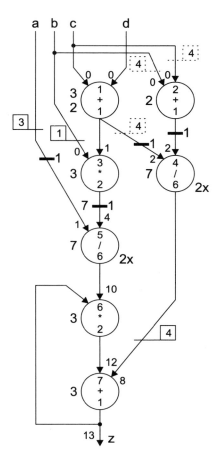

Figure 71   Illustration of the solution of Problem 3.2

For e_1, e_2, concurrence would be obtained in the case of ASAP schedule. Therefore, let the ALAP schedule be assumed:

$$\frac{0 - 4 - 2}{R} \leq K \leq \frac{0 - 4 + 3}{R}$$

The smallest R excluding the integer solution for K is 7, but $R = 8$ also does it.

For checking the pair e_2, e_7, the ALAP schedule must be applied, because it has already been assumed for e_2:

$$\frac{4-12-3}{R} \leq K \leq \frac{4-12+2}{R}$$

Now, R cannot be smaller than 12 for excluding the integer solution for K. However, this value of R would provide $K = -1$ as an integer solution for the pair e_1, e_7. Therefore, no such $R < L$ can be found by applying ALAP schedule, which would enable the allocation of all the three addition operations in a common processor. Note that $R = 16$ would exclude the integer K solutions for all the pairs simultaneously, but this restarting period is longer than the latency ($L = 13$). Anyway, after having modified the EOG by RESTART for $R = 4$, applying $R = 16$ would be beyond reason.

Generally, it cannot be excluded that a specific schedule between ASAP and ALAP may enable the allocation. In this example, however, no such schedule could be generated, which would allow allocating all addition operations in a common processor, if $R < L$.

Solution 4

1. The need for synchronizing delay effects can be decreased, if the EOG is constructed from transfer sequences having as little difference in duration as possible. For example, the left EOG in Figure 72 illustrates a solution obtained directly from the given form of the expression. In this case, the differences between the durations of transfer sequences – and so the differences between data arriving times at the inputs of the DIVISION and MULTIPLICATION – are rather large. For example, less difference can be achieved by regrouping the expression (as shown on the right side of Figure 72). Let this solution be chosen for the further calculations.

2. The only buffer insertion which makes sense is shown in Figure 73. Thus

   $$\min R = 41 + 1 = 42$$

   Synchronizing delay effect is needed at the input of e_3 only, where $\max p_{3,2} = 36$. By applying algorithm SYNC:

   $$\min p_{3,2} = 36 + 30 + 1 - 42 = 25$$

3. The restarting period is the time interval between two scans at the inputs of the datapath. Considering the length 10^{-7} s of the clock

$$f_n = f_r \cdot \frac{r - a}{r} \qquad\qquad f_n = \frac{f_r}{r} \cdot (r - a)$$

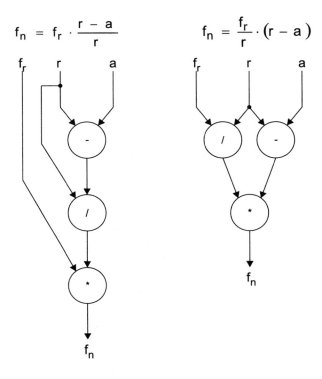

Figure 72 Illustration of the solution of Problem 4.1

period at 10 MHz, the absolute value of the restarting period $|R|$ can be obtained:

$$|R| = 42 \cdot 10^{-7} \text{ s}.$$

During this time interval, the datapath is insensible to the input changes. Knowing the maximal changing rate, the pessimistic value of sensing error can be calculated. For the input f_r, this maximal sensing error $E(f_r)$ can be obtained as follows:

$$E(f_r) = 42 \cdot 10^{-7} \text{ s} \cdot 0.1 \frac{\text{Hz}}{\text{s}} = 4.2 \cdot 10^{-7} \text{ Hz}$$

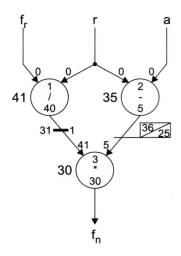

Figure 73   Illustration of the solution of Problem 4.2

Solution 5

1. In Figures 74 and 75, three possible versions of the EOG are illustrated depending on the regrouping of the original expression. The version shown in Figure 75 seems to be the most beneficial regarding the duration difference of transfer sequences, that may reduce the necessary values of synchronizing delay effects. Let this version of EOG be chosen for further calculations.

2. By buffer insertion only, the shortest restarting period achievable is 42. Only two buffers are necessary for the solution in Figure 75.

   Applying algorithm SYNC for the EOG in Figure 75:

$$\max p_{3,1} = 30; \quad \min p_{3,1} = 30 + 40 + 1 - 42 = 29$$
$$\max p_{4,f} = 5; \quad \min p_{4,f} = 5 + 30 + 1 - 42 = -6 \to 0$$

3. The mobility of e_1 is determined by $\max p_{3,1} = 30$ and e_2 has no mobility. Thus $b_2 = 0$ and b_1 is to be calculated. Applying inequality 7.2 of Chapter 7:

$$\frac{0 - b_1 - 6}{42} \leq K \leq \frac{0 - b_1 + 35}{42}$$

Even if $b_1 = 30$, the left side is negative and the right side is still positive. Therefore, the concurrence always holds, i.e., e_1 and e_2 cannot be allocated to a common functional unit.

4. The delay D_I allowed for interaction in the real-time mode is determined by the latency L of the datapath and the time T_m required for measurement:

$$D_I = T_m + L$$

must hold. In this case:

$$D_I = 0.02 \text{ ms} = 2 \cdot 10^{-5} \text{ s}$$
$$L = 76 \cdot 10^{-7} \text{ s}$$
$$T_m = D_I - L = 2 \cdot 10^{-5} - 76 \cdot 10^{-7} = 124 \cdot 10^{-7} \text{ s.}$$

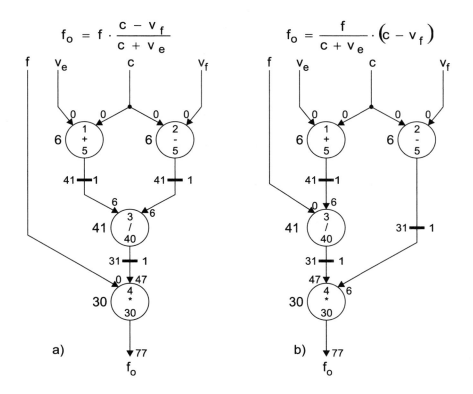

Figure 74   Illustration of the solution of Problems 5.1 and 5.2

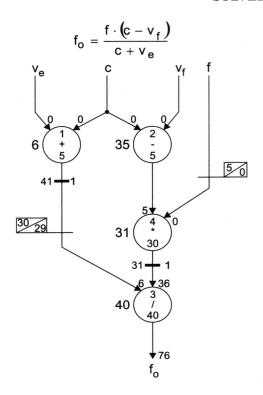

Figure 75   EOG chosen for the solution of Problems 5.1 and 5.2

5. The instruments with measuring time $T_m = 124 \cdot 10^{-7}$ s represent additional operations with duration $t_m = 124$ clock cycles at the input of the datapath. This duration causes a busy time of at least $q_m = 124 + 1 = 125$, which excludes applying $R = 42$. If no faster instruments are available, then each instrument should be replicated in

$$c_m = \left\lceil \frac{124 + 2}{42} \right\rceil = 3$$

copies.

Solution 6

The first buffer should be inserted after e_1 in the time distance:

$$R - t_1 - 2 = 6 - 2 - 2 = 2,$$

that is between e_3 and e_4, since

$$0.8 + 0.8 < 2, \quad \text{but} \quad 0.8 + 0.8 + 0.8 > 2.$$

Extra buffers should be inserted in time steps not longer than $R - 3$, thus, between e_6 and e_7, and between e_9 and e_{10}.

In this way, there is a buffer at the end of the non-synchronous sequence. Therefore, $R = 6$ is ensured anyway.

Solution 7

The first buffer should be inserted after e_1 in the time distance:

$$R - t_1 - 2 = 5 - 3 - 2 = 0,$$

which means that the first buffer should be inserted just between e_1 and e_2.

There is no need for buffer insertion inside the non-synchronous sequence, since

$$R - 3 = 5 - 3 = 2 > 0.4 + 0.4 + 0.4$$

However, an additional buffer is required between e_4 and e_5, because the busy time of the buffer placed after e_1 is

$$\left\lceil 1 + \sum_{z=2}^{4} \underline{t}_z + t_j \right\rceil = \lceil 1 + 0.4 + 0.4 + 0.4 + 2 \rceil = 5,$$

which would not allow $R = 5$.

Solution 8

For $R = 4$, e_1 must be applied in multiple copies:

$$c_1 = \left\lceil \frac{4 + 2}{4} \right\rceil = 2$$

In this case

$$c_1 \cdot R - t_1 = 2 \cdot 4 - 4 = 4 > \sum_{z=2}^{4} \underline{t}_z + t_5 = 0.4 + 0.8 + 0.4 + 1$$

holds. Therefore, there is no need for buffer insertion.

Solution 9

The transfer sequences:

$$S_{1,1} = 1, 2, 3, 4, 5, 6, 7, 8, 9$$
$$S_{1,2} = 1, 2, 3, 10$$
$$S_{1,3} = 1, 2, 3, 4, 11$$
$$S_{1,4} = 1, 2, 3, 4, 5, 12$$

For every sequence,

$$R - t_1 - 2 = 5 - 2 - 2 = 1$$

holds, therefore the first buffer must be inserted after e_3, since

$$0.4 + 0.3 < 1, \quad \text{but} \quad 0.4 + 0.3 + 0.6 > 1.$$

The next buffer in $S_{1,1}$ should be inserted after a time distance

$$R - 3 = 5 - 3 = 2,$$

that is, between e_7 and e_8, since

$$0.6 + 0.3 + 0.6 + 0.4 < 2, \quad \text{but} \quad 0.6 + 0.3 + 0.6 + 0.4 + 0.7 > 2.$$

One more buffer is necessary in $S_{1,1}$, namely after e_8, because

$$R - t_9 - 2 = 5 - 3 - 2 = 0 < \sum_{z=8}^{8} \underline{t}_z = 0.7.$$

In $S_{1,2}$,

$$\sum_{z=2}^{3} \underline{t}_z = 0.4 + 0.3 = 0.7 < R - 3 = 5 - 3 \quad \text{and}$$

$$\sum_{z=2}^{3} \underline{t}_z = 0.7 < R - t_{10} - 2 = 5 - 2 - 2 = 1$$

hold, therefore there is no need for buffer insertion.
$S_{1,3}$ also does not need extra buffers:

$$\sum_{z=4}^{4} \underline{t}_z = 0.6 < R - 3 = 5 - 3 \quad \text{and}$$

$$\sum_{z=4}^{4} \underline{t}_z = 0.6 < R - t_{11} - 2 = 5 - 2 - 2 = 1.$$

In $S_{1,4}$:

$$\sum_{z=4}^{5} t_z = 0.6 + 0.3 = 0.9 < R - 3 = 2, \quad \text{but}$$

$$\sum_{z=4}^{5} t_z = 0.9 < R - t_{12} - 2 = 5 - 2 - 2 = 1.$$

Consequently, no extra buffer is required between e_5 and e_{12}. The results are illustrated in Figure 76.

Solution 10

As illustrated on the accompanying CD-ROM, the schedule implementing the necessary hardware requires two multipliers and one each of the other processor types. Multiplier instance 0 starts in cycles 15 and 38. The second multiplier starts processing in cycles 0 and 21. The start times of the adder are 1, 16, and 33. Division starts in cycle 9, the minimum operation starts in cycle 37. (Cycles are in the overlapped time domain, i.e., between cycles 0 and R.)

Solution 11

The binary part of the EOG uses the processors for addition only. Even if the multipliers are not utilized, this is not a loss, since they are available anyway. (The implementation of linear branches requires these operations.)

The number of purely binary levels (A) is 6, since the number of operations may not exceed 18, i.e., $W = 18$. Therefore, since $W \leq 2^{A-2}$,

$$A = \lfloor \log_2 18 \rfloor + 2 = 6$$

As $W < 2^A$, the last level is not filled completely. In fact, only two of the operations on level 5 contain two direct predecessors, which increases the number of simultaneously executing processors to 18. The rest of the structure is built using linear branches, building 18 of them in parallel.

The binary part of the EOG processes only additions; the 128 multiplications must be handled by the linear branches. Since there are 18 parallel branches, the branches must handle

$$\left\lceil \frac{128}{18} \right\rceil = 8$$

terms each.

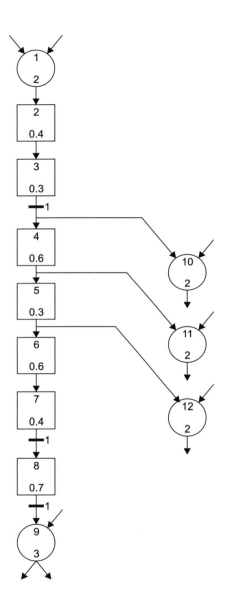

Figure 76   Illustration of the solution of Problem 9

The complete depth of the EOG in this configuration is 14, therefore, the minimum system latency is $14 \cdot 16 = 224$. Applying RESTART to the system inserts a buffer between each pair of operations, therefore, minimum latency is increased to 237 cycles.

Note: See the EOG of the structure in the "examples" directory of the CD-ROM.

16.3 Benchmark problems solved by tool PIPE

The next seven problems are widely used benchmarks for high-level synthesis. For each example, an initial EOG is given. The results produced by PIPE are illustrated as a function of the restarting period changed in its whole domain between 3 and the latency. The resulting number of processors and buffers, latency and cost are presented in diagrams and tables. The results in tables are generated in the mode of PIPE, which allows one to allocate only identical operations into common processors. However, additional busy time diagrams are also shown for some problems, which illustrate the results obtained in the PIPE mode allowing the allocation of different operations into common processors. For simplicity, the value of cost is calculated as the sum of the number of processors multiplied by their durations. Modified graphs are also given indicating buffer insertions, replicated (multiple) operation and the allocation for selected restarting periods. The selections are made in oreder to achieve local or global minimum of cost or to obtain replicated (multiple) operations or non-trivial allocation. The resulting number of buffers does not contain those synchronizing delay buffers which occur immediately at the inputs of EOGs. Thus, the proper timing of input data is supposed to be solved not necessarily by inserted buffers. However, these input delay buffers are also shown in resulting EOGs to illustrate the required input timing.

The cosine equation

The EOG (Figure 77) represents the calculation of the cosine equation:

$$p = a^2 + b^2 - 2 \cdot a \cdot b \cdot \cos \gamma.$$

In this case, the function *cos* is considered to be an elementary operation.

The durations of operations assumed for the calculation are shown in Table 7.

Table 8 illustrates the number of processors, number of buffers, latency and cost as a function of the restart period. In this and the following tables R is the restart time, *Processors* is the number of processors, *Buffers* is the number of buffers, L is the latency from the input to output and *Cost* is the total cost of the solution. The cost function is shown in Figure 78, and the modified EOG for $R = 9$ in Figure 79.

Table 7 Durations for the cosine equation

Operation	Execution time
Multiplication	8
Cosine	8
Addition	6
Subtraction	6

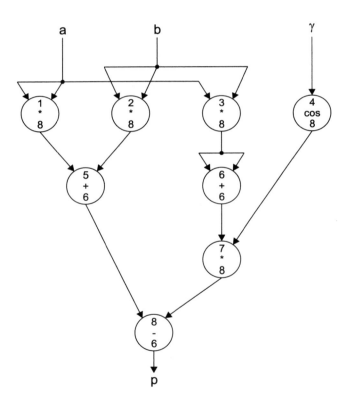

Figure 77 The EOG of the cosine equation

Table 8   Results for the cosine equation

R	Processors	cos	mul	sub	add	Buffers	Cost	L
3	31	4	16	3	8	35	261	32
4	29	4	16	3	6	36	250	32
5	24	3	12	3	6	34	208	32
6	22	3	12	1	6	36	198	32
7	18	3	12	1	2	36	174	32
8	18	3	12	1	2	36	174	32
9	8	1	4	1	2	14	72	31
10	8	1	4	1	2	14	72	31
11	8	1	4	1	2	13	71	31
12	8	1	4	1	2	9	67	31
16	8	1	4	1	2	9	67	28
17	8	1	4	1	2	15	73	28
21	8	1	4	1	2	15	73	28
22	8	1	4	1	2	8	66	28
26	8	1	4	1	2	8	66	28
27	7	1	3	1	2	7	57	28
28	7	1	3	1	2	8	58	28

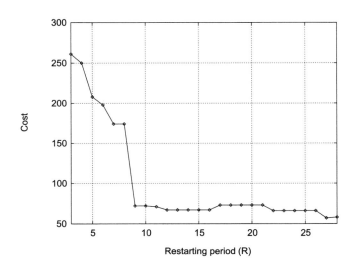

Figure 78   The cost function of the cosine equation

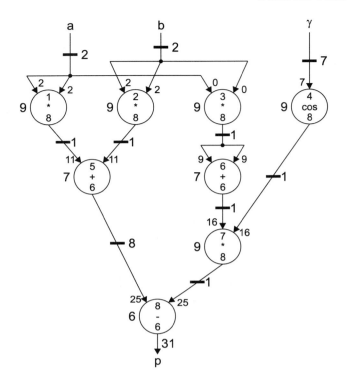

Figure 79 Modified EOG of the cosine equation for $R = 9$

Sine

This EOG represents the calculation of the sine value of input x using a Taylor-sequence approximation, based on the following equation:

$$\sin x \approx x - \frac{1}{3!} \cdot x^3 + \frac{1}{5!} \cdot x^5 - \frac{1}{7!} \cdot x^7 + \frac{1}{9!} \cdot x^9$$

Our possible EOG representation is shown in Figure 80.

The durations of operations assumed for the calculation are shown in Table 9.

Table 10 illustrates the number of processors, number of buffers and the cost as a function of the restart period.

In Figure 81 the diagram of the cost function is shown. Shaded areas in Figure 82 indicate the operations allocated into one processor.

Table 9   Durations for the sine

Operation	Execution time
Multiplication	8
Addition	4
Subtraction	4

Table 10   Results for the sine

R	Processors	add	mul	sub	Buffers	Cost	L
3	60	6	48	6	681	1113	86
4	58	4	48	6	685	1109	86
5	40	2	36	2	613	917	86
8	40	2	36	2	610	914	86
9	15	1	12	2	92	200	85
10	14	1	12	1	88	192	85
11	14	1	12	1	88	192	85
12	15	2	12	1	97	205	85
13	15	1	12	2	93	201	84
14	14	1	12	1	93	197	84
17	14	1	12	1	62	166	76
18	13	1	11	1	60	156	76
24	13	1	11	1	72	168	76
25	12	1	10	1	72	160	76
26	12	1	10	1	72	160	76
27	11	1	9	1	72	152	76
28	10	1	8	1	72	144	76
31	10	1	8	1	72	144	76
32	8	1	6	1	72	128	76
37	8	1	6	1	72	128	76
38	9	1	7	1	72	136	76
39	8	1	6	1	72	128	76
40	8	1	6	1	72	128	76
41	7	1	5	1	72	120	76
56	7	1	5	1	72	120	76
57	6	1	4	1	72	112	76
63	6	1	4	1	72	112	76
64	5	1	3	1	72	104	76
76	5	1	3	1	72	104	76

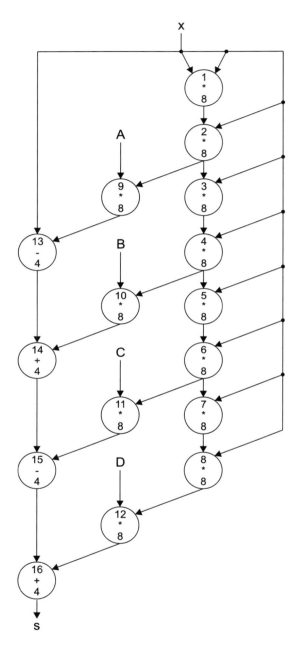

Figure 80   One possible EOG representation of sine

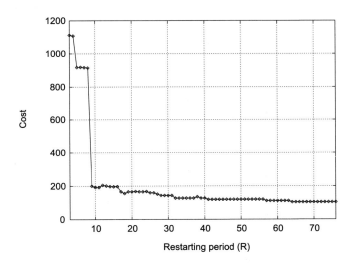

Figure 81   Cost vs. restarting period of the sine approximation

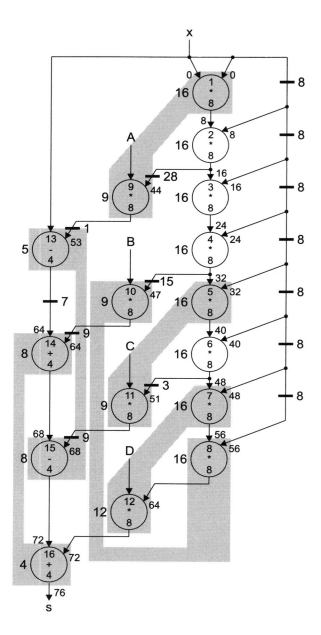

Figure 82   Modified EOG of sine for $R = 28$

Edge detection using Laplace operation

The EOG represents an image processing algorithm, the edge detection. This method is based on the second derivative of the intensity. This is done by the convolution of the image with the following matrix:

$$\begin{bmatrix} 0 & 1 & 0 \\ 1 & -4 & 1 \\ 0 & 1 & 0 \end{bmatrix},$$

that is with the graph inputs:

$$\begin{bmatrix} 0 & x_0 & 0 \\ x_1 & -4 \cdot x_4 & x_2 \\ 0 & x_3 & 0 \end{bmatrix}$$

Two possible EOGs are shown in Figures 83 and 84. The cost function is shown in Figure 85.

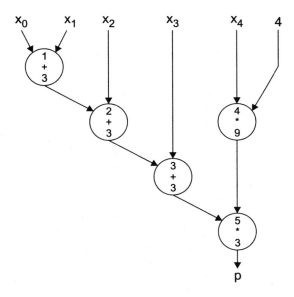

Figure 83 EOG for Laplace operation *(graph 1)*

The durations assumed for the calculation are shown in Table 11.

Tables 12 and 13 illustrate the number of processors, number of buffers and the cost as a function of the restart period for both EOGs, respectively.

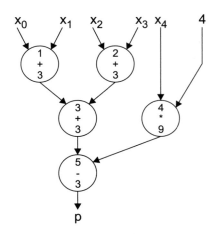

Figure 84   Alternative EOG for Laplace operation *(graph 2)*

Table 11   Durations for Laplace operation

Operation	Execution time
Multiplication	9
Addition	3
Subtraction	3

Table 12   Results for Laplace operation *(graph 1)*

R	Processors	add	mul	sub	Buffers	Cost	L
3	15	9	5	1	22	97	16
4	8	3	4	1	6	54	15
5	7	3	3	1	6	45	15
6	7	3	3	1	6	45	15
7	7	3	3	1	4	43	14
8	6	2	3	1	4	40	14
9	6	2	3	1	4	40	14
10	4	2	1	1	2	20	13
11	4	2	1	1	2	20	13
12	4	2	1	1	2	20	13

Table 13   Results for Laplace operation *(graph 2)*

R	Processors	add	mul	sub	Buffers	Cost	L
3	15	9	5	1	11	86	14
4	8	3	4	1	5	53	14
5	7	3	3	1	7	46	14
6	7	3	3	1	8	47	14
7	7	3	3	1	8	47	14
8	6	2	3	1	8	44	14
9	6	2	3	1	8	44	14
10	4	2	1	1	6	24	13
11	4	2	1	1	6	24	13
12	4	2	1	1	5	23	13

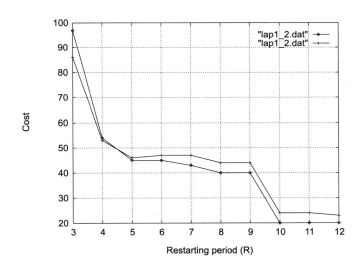

Figure 85   Cost vs. restarting period for the two forms of
Laplace operation

Shaded areas in Figure 86 indicate the operations allocated into one
processor.

The modified EOG for $R = 5$ is shown in Figure 87.

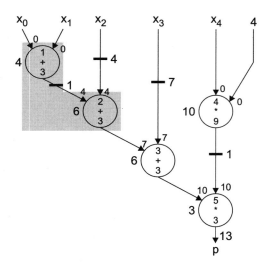

Figure 86   Modified EOG of Laplace for $R = 12$

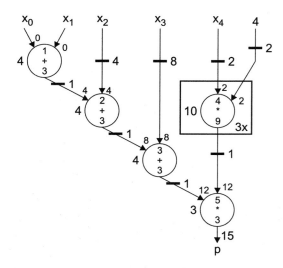

Figure 87   Modified EOG of Laplace for $R = 5$, with a multiple (replicated) operation

The FFT

The EOG representing the FFT *(Fast Fourier Transformation)* consists of similar blocks of multipliers, adders and subtractors connected as shown in Figure 88. Inputs W are constants.

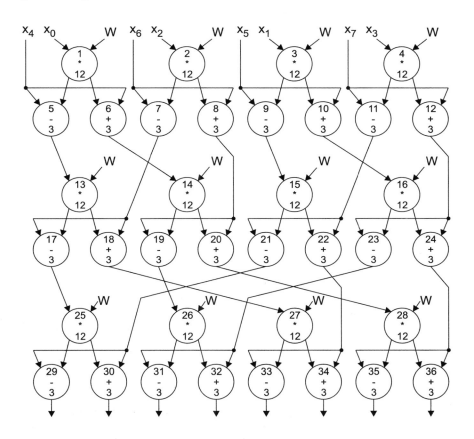

Figure 88   The graph of an FFT block

The durations assumed for the calculation are shown in Table 14.

The results are shown for one output in Table 15 and in Figure 89. The results are the same for each output.

Figure 90 shows the modified EOG for $R = 30$. Shaded areas indicate the operations allocated into one processor.

The busy time diagrams are shown in Figures 91 and 92.

Table 14 Durations for FFT

Operation	Execution time
Multiplication	12
Addition	3
Subtraction	3

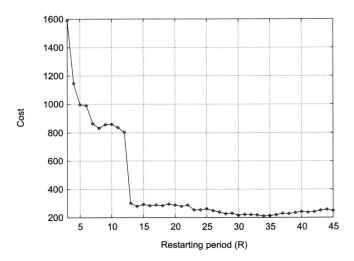

Figure 89 Cost vs. restarting period for FFT

Table 15   Cost, processors, buffers and latency vs. restarting period of FFT

R	Processors	add	mul	sub	Buffers	Cost	L
3	128	28	72	28	559	1591	51
4	84	12	60	12	356	1148	51
5	72	12	48	12	348	996	51
6	72	12	48	12	342	990	51
7	52	8	36	8	384	864	51
8	50	7	36	7	358	832	51
9	50	7	36	7	383	857	51
10	48	6	36	6	392	860	51
11	48	6	36	6	369	837	51
12	46	5	36	5	342	804	51
13	20	4	12	4	132	300	50
14	24	6	12	6	99	279	50
15	24	6	12	6	112	292	50
16	26	7	12	7	96	282	45
17	26	7	12	7	102	288	45
18	22	5	12	5	109	283	45
19	24	6	12	6	114	294	45
21	24	6	12	6	99	279	45
22	22	5	12	5	114	288	45
25	22	5	12	5	87	261	45
26	22	6	11	5	83	248	45
27	21	5	11	5	76	238	45
29	21	5	11	5	68	230	45
30	19	5	9	5	78	216	45
32	19	5	9	5	82	220	45
33	17	4	9	4	86	218	45
34	16	4	8	4	90	210	45
37	16	4	8	4	109	229	45
38	15	4	7	4	119	227	45
40	15	4	7	4	133	241	45
41	14	4	6	4	140	236	45
44	14	4	6	4	160	256	45
45	13	4	5	4	164	248	45

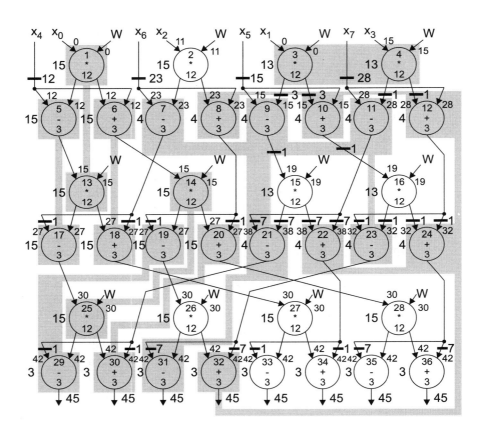

Figure 90 Modified EOG of FFT for $R = 30$

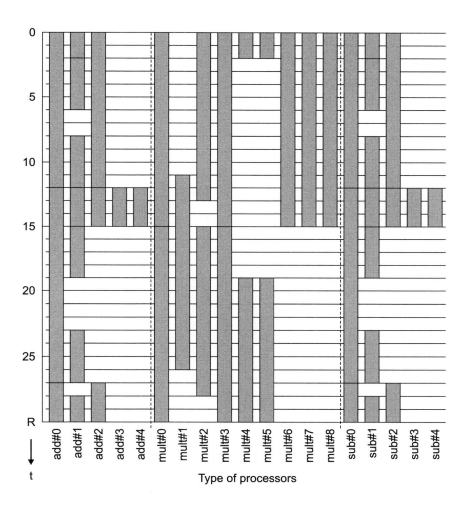

Figure 91 Busy time diagram of FFT for $R = 30$ (identical
operations in common processors)

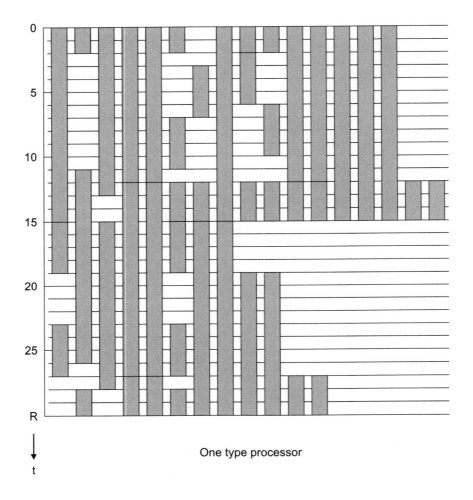

One type processor

Figure 92   Busy time diagram of FFT for $R = 30$ (different
operations allowed in common processors)

The Fifth Order Elliptical Wave Filter

The EOG representing the elliptic filter — an Infinite Impulse Response (IIR) filter — consists of multipliers and adders connected as shown in Figure 93. Inputs $i_1 \ldots i_8$ are constants.

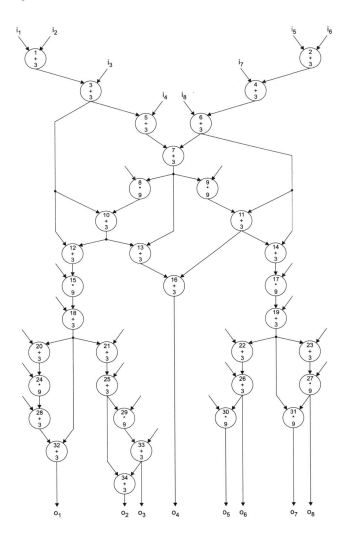

Figure 93 The EOG of fifth order elliptical wave filter

The durations assumed for the calculation are shown in Table 16.

Table 16 Durations for IIR filter

Operation	Execution time
Multiplication	9
Addition	3

The results are shown in Table 17 and in Figure 94.
Figure 95 shows the modified EOG for $R = 24$.
The busy time diagrams are shown in Figures 96 and 97.

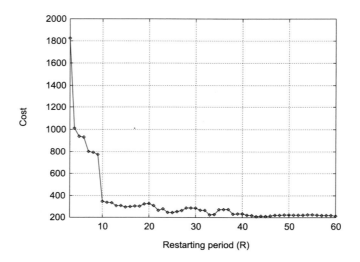

Figure 94 Cost vs. restart time for IIR filter

Table 17 Results for IIR filter

R	Processors	add	mul	Buffers	Cost	L
3	109	70	39	1264	1825	74
4	58	26	32	645	1011	73
5	50	26	24	645	939	73
6	49	25	24	641	932	73
7	46	22	24	519	801	66
8	43	19	24	520	793	66
9	39	17	22	525	774	66
10	23	15	8	230	347	66
11	22	14	8	223	337	66
13	22	14	8	192	306	60
15	22	14	8	180	294	60
16	23	15	8	181	298	60
17	23	15	8	186	303	60
20	19	11	8	221	326	60
22	16	9	7	174	264	60
23	18	10	8	176	278	60
24	13	8	5	176	245	60
26	15	9	6	172	253	60
27	14	9	5	191	263	60
30	13	7	6	210	285	60
40	15	9	6	152	233	60
42	12	7	5	152	218	60
43	11	7	4	152	209	60
45	10	6	4	156	210	60
46	11	7	4	157	214	60
49	12	8	4	164	224	60
56	11	7	4	165	222	60
57	10	6	4	165	219	60
60	8	4	4	165	213	60

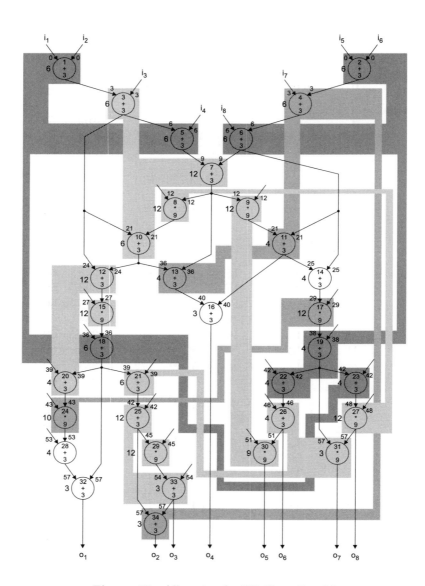

Figure 95 Allocation for IIR filter, $R = 24$

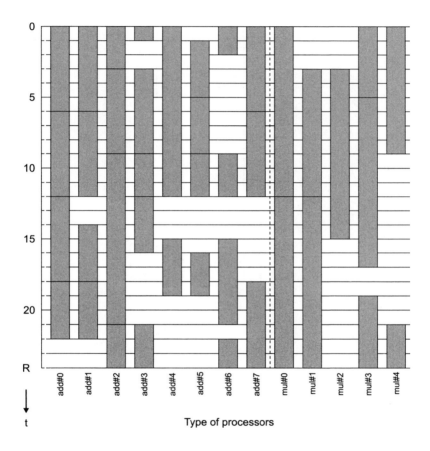

Figure 96 Busy time diagram of IIR filter for $R = 24$ (identical operations in common processors)

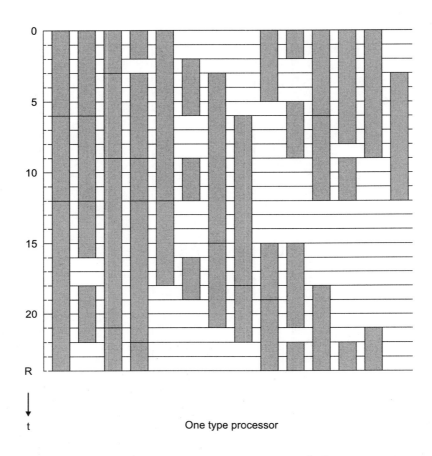

One type processor

Figure 97   Busy time diagram of IIR filter for $R = 24$ (different operations allowed in common processors)

The IDEA cipher

The IDEA cipher performs the encryption/decryption of data streams in a communications line.

The EOG of the IDEA cipher consists of several similar blocks connected in cascade. Each block processes a part of the clear text (inputs p_x) and a segment of the key (inputs s_x) (Figure 98).

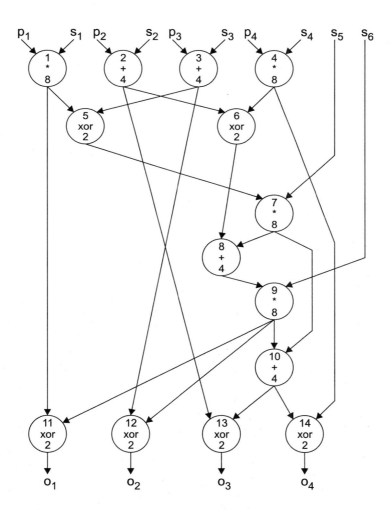

Figure 98 The EOG of an IDEA block

The durations assumed for the calculation are shown in Table 18, and the cost function is shown in Figure 99. Results are shown in Table 19.
The busy time diagrams are shown in Figures 100 and 101.

Table 18   Durations for IDEA cipher

Operation	Execution time
Multiplication	8
Addition	4
XOR	2

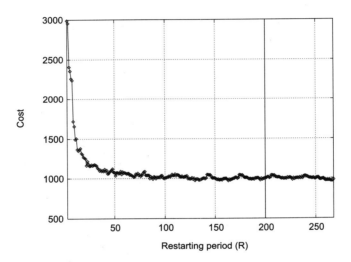

Figure 99   Cost vs. restart time for IDEA cipher

Table 19   Results for IDEA cipher

R	Processors	add	mul	xor	Buffers	Cost	L
3	286	102	136	48	1397	2989	325
4	280	98	134	48	1395	2955	325
5	184	34	102	48	1360	2408	325
6	160	34	102	24	1357	2357	325
7	162	34	102	26	1257	2261	317
8	155	33	98	24	1276	2240	317
9	88	32	34	22	1271	1715	316
10	75	23	34	18	1253	1653	316
13	80	22	34	24	960	1368	268
17	73	19	32	22	940	1316	268
18	67	17	29	21	961	1303	268
20	60	15	28	17	940	1258	268
24	47	13	18	16	948	1176	268
32	50	10	18	22	930	1158	268
35	35	10	13	12	927	1095	268
42	29	8	12	9	954	1100	268
52	24	6	9	9	957	1071	268
67	22	6	8	8	932	1036	268
75	20	5	8	7	944	1042	268
122	16	4	6	6	954	1030	268
132	14	3	6	5	923	993	268
154	10	2	4	4	932	980	268
162	13	3	4	6	929	985	268
200	13	4	4	5	946	1004	268
221	12	3	4	5	942	996	268
247	9	3	3	3	960	1002	268
248	10	3	4	3	955	1005	268
249	8	2	3	3	956	994	268
257	10	3	4	3	944	994	268
260	8	2	3	3	935	973	268
268	7	2	2	3	952	982	268

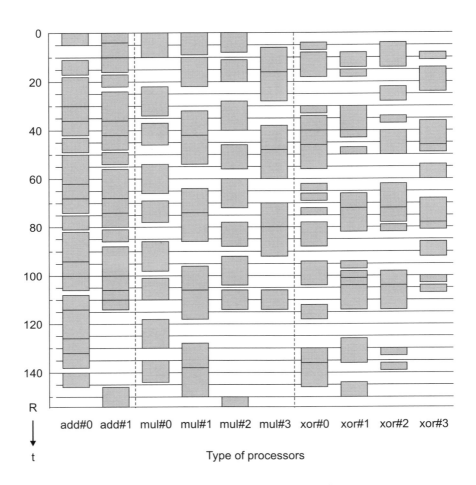

Figure 100 Busy time diagram of IDEA for $R = 154$ (identical operations
in common processors)

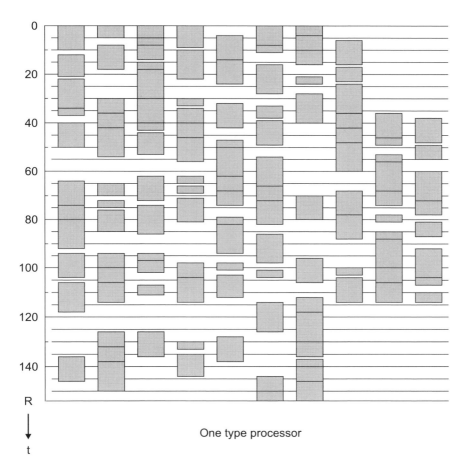

Figure 101 Busy time diagram of IDEA for $R = 154$ (different operations
allowed in common processors)

The RC6 cipher

RC6 is a fully parametrized family of encryption algorithms. A version of
RC6 is more accurately specified as RC6-$w/r/b$ where the word size is w
bits, encryption consists of a non-negative number of rounds r, and b denotes
the length of the encryption key in bytes (see Figure 102). Since the *AES*
submission is targeted at $w = 32$ and $r = 20$, we shall use the RC6 as
shorthand to refer to such versions.

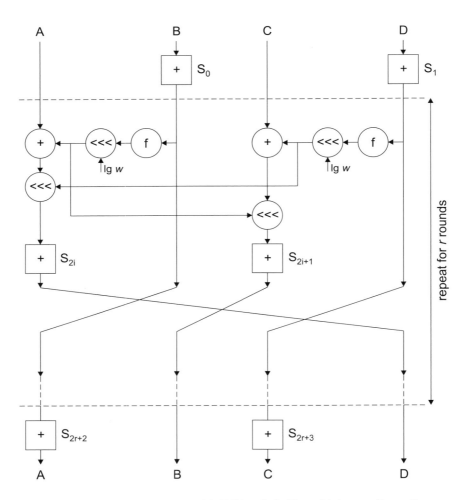

Figure 102   Encryption with RC6-$w/r/b$. Here $f(x) = x \cdot (2x + 1)$

The durations assumed for the calculation are shown in Table 20.

Table 20 Durations for RC6 cipher

Operation	Execution time
Multiplication	3
Addition	1
XOR	1
Left-rotation	1

The results are shown for one output in Table 21 and in Figure 103. The busy time diagrams are shown in Figures 104 and 105.

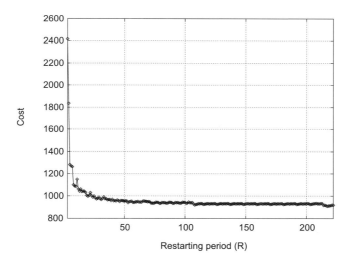

Figure 103 Cost vs. restarting period for RC6 cipher

Table 21   Results for RC6 cipher

R	Processors	add	mul	rot	xor	Buffers	Cost	L
3	442	82	240	80	40	1494	2416	302
4	182	42	80	40	20	1494	1836	302
5	222	82	80	40	20	900	1282	222
6	204	80	80	28	16	906	1270	222
7	204	80	80	28	16	899	1263	222
8	120	42	40	24	14	899	1099	222
9	112	42	40	20	10	896	1088	222
10	108	40	40	20	8	897	1085	222
11	162	42	40	40	40	907	1149	222
12	92	32	32	20	8	905	1061	222
13	80	28	28	16	8	906	1042	222
18	76	28	28	12	8	900	1032	222
19	58	20	20	12	6	907	1005	222
22	82	22	20	20	20	907	1029	222
27	44	16	16	8	4	897	973	222
33	56	14	14	14	14	907	991	222
34	42	14	14	10	4	905	975	222
37	34	12	12	6	4	909	967	222
46	26	10	10	4	2	904	950	222
53	22	8	8	4	2	902	940	222
55	34	10	8	8	8	901	951	222
63	22	8	8	4	2	908	946	222
66	32	8	8	8	8	907	955	222
74	18	6	6	4	2	905	935	222
112	14	4	4	4	2	908	930	222
125	12	4	4	2	2	911	931	222
131	16	4	4	4	4	905	929	222
158	12	4	4	2	2	911	931	222
175	16	4	4	4	4	905	929	222
217	10	4	2	2	2	895	909	222
222	8	2	2	2	2	907	919	222

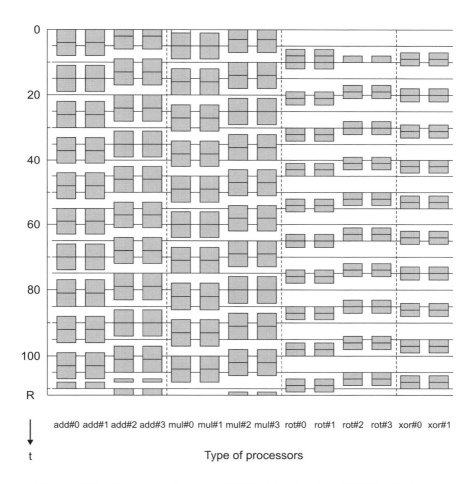

Figure 104 Busy time diagram of RC6 cipher for $R = 112$ (identical operations in common processors)

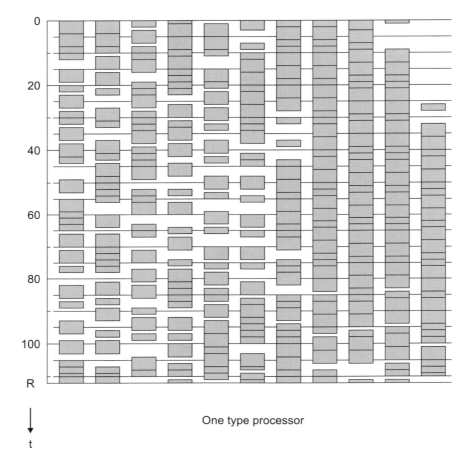

One type processor

Figure 105 Busy time diagram of RC6 cipher for $R = 112$ (different operations allowed in common processors)

The MARS cipher

MARS is a shared-key block cipher, with a block size of 128 bits and a variable key size, ranging from 128 to over 400 bits. The main theme behind the design of MARS is to get the best security/performance tradeoff by utilizing the strongest tools and techniques available today for designing block ciphers. The general structure of the cipher is depicted in Figure 106.

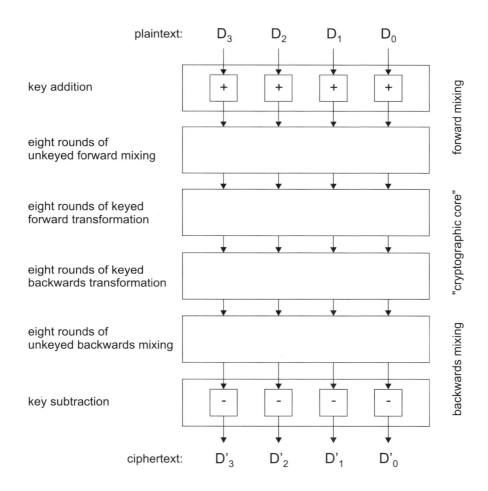

Figure 106   High-level structure of the cipher

The durations assumed for the calculation are shown in Table 22.
The results are shown for one output in Table 23 and in Figure 107.

Table 22   Durations for MARS cipher

Operation	Execution time
Multiplication	3
Addition	1
Subtraction	1
XOR	1
Right-rotation by 8 (shr8)	1
Data-dependent rotation (shl)	1
Left-rotation by 5 (shl5)	1
Left-rotation by 8 (shl8)	1
Left-rotation by 13 (shl13)	1
SBOX	1
SBOX0	1
SBOX1	1

The busy time diagrams are shown in Figures 108 and 109.

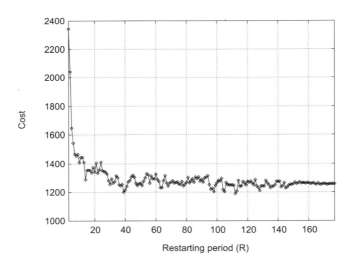

Figure 107   Cost vs. restarting period for MARS cipher

Table 23 Results for MARS cipher

R	Processors	add	mul	sbox	sbox0	sbox1	shl	shl13	shl5	shl8	shr8	sub	xor	Buffers	Cost	L
3	444	72	48	16	32	32	32	32	32	24	24	20	80	1802	2342	207
4	218	36	16	8	16	17	16	16	16	13	12	12	40	1791	2041	207
5	231	37	16	8	16	16	17	24	17	13	13	11	43	1383	1646	177
6	172	24	16	7	13	12	12	17	14	9	9	8	31	1340	1544	177
7	173	25	16	6	11	12	12	19	20	9	8	8	27	1263	1468	177
8	132	21	8	5	10	11	10	13	9	7	7	7	24	1308	1456	177
9	141	21	12	5	9	9	9	13	20	8	7	6	22	1302	1467	177
10	115	18	8	5	8	8	8	11	10	8	7	6	20	1278	1409	177
11	108	17	8	4	8	7	8	11	8	7	6	5	18	1322	1446	177
12	102	15	8	3	8	8	7	10	8	6	5	6	18	1328	1446	177
13	95	15	7	4	7	7	7	9	8	6	6	4	15	1301	1410	177
18	84	12	7	3	5	5	5	8	11	5	6	5	12	1238	1336	177
19	76	12	6	3	5	5	5	7	7	5	4	5	12	1286	1374	177
22	66	10	5	3	4	5	4	6	6	4	4	4	11	1257	1333	177
27	60	8	5	2	4	4	4	5	6	4	3	3	10	1271	1341	177
33	48	8	4	2	4	3	3	5	9	3	2	3	7	1217	1273	177
34	48	6	4	2	4	4	3	4	4	3	3	3	8	1259	1315	177
37	51	6	4	2	4	4	3	5	4	3	3	4	7	1186	1245	177
46	45	6	3	2	4	4	3	4	6	3	3	3	6	1253	1304	177
53	45	6	3	1	4	4	3	4	5	3	2	4	6	1249	1300	177
55	41	5	3	2	3	3	3	4	5	3	2	3	6	1274	1321	177
63	41	5	3	1	3	3	3	4	4	3	2	3	6	1184	1231	177
66	41	6	3	1	3	3	3	4	4	3	3	3	6	1268	1315	177
74	38	4	2	1	4	4	3	3	4	3	3	3	5	1229	1271	177
112	30	4	2	1	2	2	2	3	2	3	2	3	4	1156	1190	177
125	33	4	2	1	2	3	2	3	2	4	2	3	5	1250	1287	177
131	32	4	2	1	2	3	2	3	2	3	2	3	5	1206	1242	177
158	33	2	2	1	4	4	2	3	2	3	3	3	4	1224	1261	177
167	29	2	2	1	3	3	2	3	2	3	2	3	3	1223	1256	177
177	27	2	2	1	2	2	2	3	2	3	2	3	3	1226	1257	177

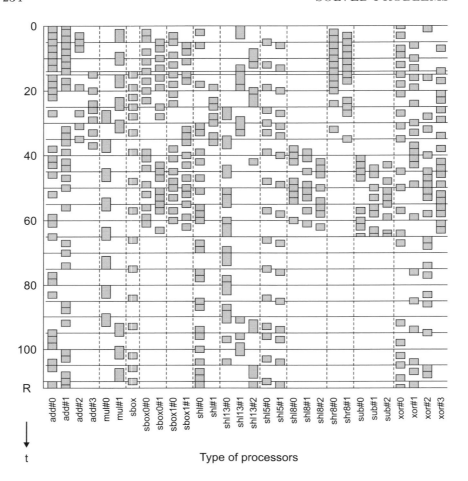

Figure 108 Busy time diagram of MARS cipher for $R = 112$ (identical operations in common processors)

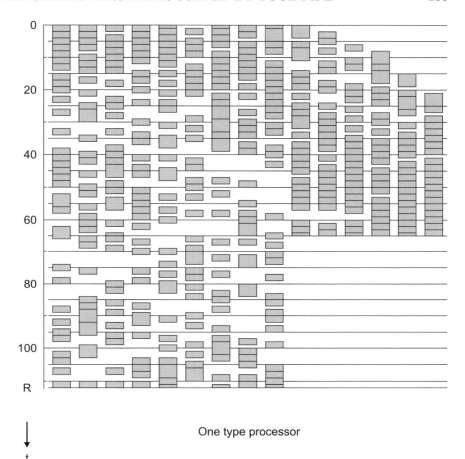

Figure 109 Busy time diagram of MARS cipher for $R = 112$ (different
operations allowed in common processors)

Further reading

Further reading in system-level synthesis

The partitioning problem may be solved at a very high level of abstraction [VG92]. To achieve the necessary abstraction level, problem descriptions are not expanded to implementation details. System descriptions at this level are strictly functional, without specifying the underlying structure. A useful tool of this approach is *behavioural-level VHDL* as a modelling language. (Behavioural-level VHDL, as opposed to structural-level VHDL, describes only the functionality of VHDL modules.) High-level partitioning is performed at the *functionality level* [GVNG98], and the corresponding partitioning problem is described as *Specification Partitioning* [VG92]. Optimization at a very high level may result in inefficiencies at lower levels. (This may not be a serious limitation in some systems, since available transistor count has been increasing faster than designer productivity [Wir98, VG99].)

Functional partitioning makes it possible to partition software components among several processors, an advantage not present in most other practically used hardware-software codesign methods. In addition to the requirements of multiprocessor software implementations, functional partitioning enables design reuse. Extending already existing systems is also easier, since the existing modules need to be described in high-level languages (i.e., behavioural VHDL, Java or C) [Dew97].

An additional advantage of a higher-level description of system functionality is the ability to perform incremental performance approximations in the design flow. Since most partitioning steps relocate only a limited set of operations between different execution contexts, usually a small subset of performance metrics has to be recomputed between iterations. Structural partitioning techniques with incremental evaluation report impressive performance improvements in systems where changes between iterations are most likely to be gradual [VG95].

The Oxford University Computing Laboratory does not try to handle the hardware-software codesign design process as a traditional development cycle. Since their synthesis process generates a custom "microprocessor" in reprogrammable hardware units, an already existing microprocessor framework is required to avoid extremely long synthesis cycles. This approach may increase the ratio of wasted silicon to a very high level, especially in smaller designs.

Because the Oxford University Computing Laboratory researchers do not wish to make a clean distinction between hardware and software as target systems, the laboratory has a slightly different approach to system descriptions than is generally accepted. Instead of relying on VHDL descriptions for hardware and C code for software subsystems (or combination thereof), the laboratory strictly enforces the policy of using a common description language to cover problems [Pag95a]. The programming language *Handel*, a derivative of *occam*, is a deliberately spartan subset of functionality (the only exception being type conversion, which has extensive support to reduce hardware waste). By providing less comfort for designers, the Handel environment reduces the burden on optimization, and decreases compiler complexity considerably. Creating a higher level of abstraction and additional optimization steps in the Handel compiler is a future development plan of the laboratory.

Research groups at the University of Washington have investigated the partitioning problem in soft-programmable FPGA structures. Expecting the advances in FPGA technologies, extensive benchmarking and algorithm development was targeted in the early nineties, while FPGA implementations became capable of building the required complex structures only recently. The inherent problems of unpredictable propagation times inside FPGA packages change the focus of the partitioning process somewhat. In addition to multiple restrictions on system topologies and limitations on the number of signal propagation levels, highly nonlinear (exponential) timing penalties have to be introduced to graph cuts [HB95b]. The high penalty values are caused by the exponential increase in delays (load capacitances) when signals are leaving and entering FPGA packages. In addition to the differences between internal and external propagation delays, delays inside packages depend on compilation circumstances and may be difficult to predict in most practical systems. Even if recent advances in FPGA routing technologies decrease the standard deviation of internal propagation delay distributions, FPGA timings should not be modelled as fixed values.

The University of Washington research results include detailed analysis of partitioning algorithms adapted to supercomputing [HB95a] and hardware systems with multiple FPGAs [HB95b].

Further reading in methodology

R. Camposano and W. Wolf. *High-Level VLSI Synthesis*. Kluwer Academic Publishers, 1991.

D. Gajski. *High-Level Synthesis*. Kluwer Academic Publishers, 1992.

A. A. Jerraya. *Behavioural Synthesis and Component Reuse with VHDL*. Kluwer Academic Publishers, 1997.

A. A. Jerraya and J. Mermet. *System-Level Synthesis* (NATO science series). Kluwer Academic Publishers, 1998.

G. De Micheli. *Synthesis and Optimization of Digital Circuits*. McGraw-Hill, 1994.

Further reading in software performance optimization

Neal Margulis. Programming RISC engines. *Doctor Dobb's Journal*, February 1990.

Ramesh Subramaniam and Kiran Kundargi. Programming the Pentium processor. *Doctor Dobb's Journal*, June 1993.

Mike Schmit. Optimizing Pentium code. *Doctor Dobb's Journal*, January 1994.

Further reading in processor realizations

PowerPC 604 RISC Microprocessor Technical Summary. Order number MPC604/D. Motorola Inc., 1994.

Glossary

ALAP: As Late As Possible. Scheduling term for the latest time cycle when an elementary operation may start processing its input. Delaying the start of data processing after the ALAP time of an operation violates maximum system latency constraints.

Approximation Algorithm: Polynomial-time solutions of minimization or maximization problems that have a guaranteed bound on the ratio between the worst case solution cost and the optimum solution cost.

ASAP: As Soon As Possible. Scheduling term for the earliest time cycle when an elementary operation may start processing its input. Processing may not start before the ASAP cycle since data on operation inputs may not be stable before that time.

ASIC: Application-Specific Integrated Circuit. Custom integrated circuits designed to solve specific problems. ASICs are more efficient than commercial, general-purpose designs at the expense of extended development time and higher cost.

CDFG: Control-Data-Flow Graph. A graphical representation of data propagation inside a system. Operations are data operations; edges are data connections. The system contains additional information from which control structures may be generated.

CFG: Control-Flow Graph. A graphical representation of control information inside a system.

DAG: Directed Acyclic Graph. A directed graph without cycles, representing data transfers and operations in HLS. Usually used as a synonym of DFG in system-level synthesis context.

DFG: Data-Flow Graph. A graphical representation of data propagation inside a system. Graph operations are data operations; edges represent data transfers.

EEOG: Extended Elementary Operation Graph. An EOG describing system functionality as a set of non-elementary operations. EEOG operations may be decomposed to more than one primitive of the underlying RTL library.

EOG: Elementary Operation Graph. An EOG describing system functionality as a set of elementary operations. Unlike an EEOG, EOG operations are implemented as a single primitive of the underlying RTL library.

HDL: Hardware Description Language. High-level programming languages and descriptions used as sources to generate ("synthesize") hardware systems.

HSCD: Hardware-Software Co-Design.

IP: Intellectual Property (block). Generic term for standalone off-the-shelf submodules in synthesizable software/high-level descriptions (soft IP), technology-independent netlists (firm IP) or technology-specific layouts (hard IP). IP blocks may be integrated to custom designs through standardized interfaces. IP blocks typically implement standalone functions in a reusable, modular way.

Loop unrolling: A compiler optimization technique for loop constructs. Improves compiled code properties by replicating the instructions in a loop, reducing loop overhead, and increasing potential instruction-level parallelism.

MCCDFG: Multiple-Context Control-Data-Flow Graph. A graphical representation of data in multiple-context environments. MCCDFGs represent problems where solutions are generated in different execution contexts. Example execution content groups are hardware and software, multiple hardware (processor-coprocessor), multiple software (multiple CPUs, MIMD or SIMD) environments, or combinations thereof.

MCE: Multiple-Context Environment. Target systems where functional units are mapped to several disjoint, architecturally or fundamentally different *execution contexts* necessitating additional lower-level modules for communication between them. Examples are hardware-software codesign (software, hardware) or multiprocessor systems (software, software).

MCHLS: Multiple-Context High-Level Synthesis. Application of High-Level Synthesis techniques to generate systems where the target technology includes both hardware and software components.

PIPE: A High-Level Synthesis CAD tool developed at BME (Technical University of Budapest, Hungary). The tool is capable of synthesizing pipelined hardware systems (hence the name).

Recursion: A class of functions (or procedures in programming) where results are produced by the function using a value returned by repeated calls of the same function (for subproblems of smaller sizes).

RTL: Register Transfer Level. An intermediate-level description of hardware systems. RTL descriptions capture system properties as a set of registers, basic arithmetic units (ALUs), control flow (transfer sequences and conditional execution), interconnect network, elementary binary functions, and system hierarchy.

SLS: System-Level Synthesis. The procedure of generating complete systems as an integrated design process, as opposed to non-integrated, lower-level procedures.

VHDL: VHSIC (Very High Speed Integrated Circuit) HDL. A standardized HDL with different levels of abstraction, usable both for simulations and for direct hardware synthesis.

References

[AB96] P. Arató and I. Béres. A compatibility-based allocation method in high-level synthesis. *Periodica Polytechnica*, 1996.

[ABIC⁺98] Mohamed Abid, T. Ben Ismail, A. Changuel, C.A. Calderram, M. Romdhani, G.F. Marchioro, J.M. Daveau, and Ahmed A. Jerraya. A hardware-software co-design methodology for design of embedded systems. *Integrated Computer-Aided Engineering*, pages 69–83, March 1998.

[ABR⁺94] P. Arató, I. Béres, A. Rucinski, R. Davis, and R. Torbert. A high-level datapath synthesis method for pipelined structures. *Microelectronics Journal*, 25:237–247, 1994.

[AJ97] Mohamed Abid and Ahmed Jerraya. Towards hardware-software co-design: A case study of robot arm controller. *Journal of Microelectronics System Integration*, 5:167–182, 1997.

[AL98] Cleve Ashcraft and Joseph W. H. Liu. Applications of Dulmage-Mendelsohn decomposition and network flow to graph bisection improvement. *SIAM Journal on Matrix Analysis and Applications*, pages 325–354, 1998.

[ASU88] Alfred Aho, Ravi Sethi, and Jeffrey Ullman. *Compilers, Principles, and Tools*. Addison-Wesley, Reading, MA, second edition, 1988.

[AV98] Péter Arató and Tamás Visegrády. Effective graph generation from VHDL structures. *Microelectronics Journal*, 29, March 1998.

[Bor00] J. Borel. The MEDEA design automation roadmap. www.medea.org, March 2000.

[Cam90] R. Camposano. From behaviour to structure: high-level synthesis. *IEEE Design and Test of Computers*, 10:8–19, 1990.

[CR89] R. Camposano and W. Rosenstiel. Synthesizing circuits from behavioural descriptions. *IEEE Transactions on Computer Aided Design*, 2:171–180, 1989.

[Dew97] Allen Dewey. *Analysis and Design of Digital Systems with VHDL*. PWS Publishing, Boston, MA, 1997.

[FM82] Charles M. Fiduccia and R. M. Mattheyses. A linear-time heuristic for improving network partitions. In *Proceedings of the ACM/IEEE Design Automation Conference*, 1982.

[GJ79] Michael R. Garey and David S. Johnson. *Computers and Intractability: A Guide to the Theory of NP-Completeness*. W. H. Freeman, 1979.

[GVNG98] Daniel D. Gajski, Frank Vahid, Sanjiv Narayan, and Jie Gong. SpecSyn: An environment supporting the specify-explore-refine paradigm for hardware/software system design. *Transactions on VLSI Systems*, 6:84–100, 1998.

[HB95a] Scott Hauck and Gateano Borriello. An evaluation of bipartitioning techniques. In *Proceedings of the Chapel Hill Conference on Advanced Research in VLSI*, 1995.

[HB95b] Scott Hauck and Gateano Borriello. Logic partition ordering for multi-FPGA systems. In *Proceedings of the International Symposium on Field-Programmable Gate Arrays*, 1995.

[HLH91] C.-T. Hwang, J.-H. Lee, and Y.-C. Hsu. A formal approach to the scheduling problem in high-level synthesis. *IEEE Transactions on Computer Aided Design*, April 1991.

[Hoc97] Dorit S. Hochbaum, editor. *Approximation Algorithms for NP-Hard Problems*. PWS Publishing, Boston, MA, 1997.

[IEE88] IEEE. *IEEE Standard VHDL Reference Manual*. IEEE, 1988.

[IEE93] IEEE. Special issue on high-level synthesis. *IEEE Transactions on Very Large Scale Integration Systems*, 1(3), September 1993.

[JRV+98] Ahmed A. Jerraya, M. Romdhani, C. Valderrama, Ph. Le Marrec, F. Hessel, G. Marchioro, and J. Daveau. Models and languages for system-level specification and design. In *NATO ASI on System-Level Synthesis, Proceedings*, 1998.

[KL70] Brian W. Kernighan and S. Lin. An efficient heuristic procedure for partitioning electrical circuits. *Bell System Technical Journal*, 49:291–307, February 1970.

[Knu95] Peter Voigt Knudsen. Fine-grain partitioning in codesign. Master's thesis, Technical University of Denmark, Lyngby, 1995.

[Kun82] H. T. Kung. Why systolic architectures? *IEEE Computer*, 15(1):37–46, January 1982.

[Lan91] Béla Lantos. *Robotok irányítása*. Akadémiai Kiadó, Budapest, 1991.

[Las93] Gregor von Laszewski. A collection of graph partitioning algorithms. Technical report, Northeast Parallel Architectures Center, Syracuse University, NY, May 1993.

[Lip91] H. M. Lipp. Entwurf digitaler schaltungen-formale hilfsmittel. Technical report, Institut für Technik der Informationsverarbeitung, Technical University of Karlsruhe, 1991.

[MR92] P. Marwedel and W. Rosenstiel. Synthese von rt-strukturen aus verhaltensbeschreibungen. *Informatik Spektrum*, 15:454–460, 1992.

[NP95] Cindy Norris and Lori L. Pollock. An experimental study of several cooperative register allocation and instruction scheduling strategies. In *MICRO-2*, pages 28–33, November 1995.

[NP98] Cindy Norris and Lori L. Pollock. Experiences with cooperating register allocation and instruction scheduling. *International Journal on Parallel Programming*, 26:241–284, September 1998.

[Pag94] Ian Page. Automatic design and implementation of microprocessors. In *Proceedings of WoTUG (World occam and Transputer User Group) '94*, 1994.

[Pag95a] Ian Page. Constructing hardware-software systems from a single description. Technical report, Oxford Hardware Compilation Research Group, July 1995.

[Pag95b] Ian Page. Reconfigurable processor architectures. *Microprocessors and Microsystems (special issue on Hardware/Software Codesign)*, April 1995.

[Pin96] Randall D. Pinkett. Hardware/software co-design and digital signal processing. Master's thesis, University of Oxford, May 1996.

[PK89] P. G. Paulin and J. P. Knight. Force-directed scheduling for the behavioural synthesis of ASICs. *IEEE Transactions on Computer Aided Design*, 1989.

[PP86] N. Park and A. Parker. Shewa: A program for synthesis of pipelines. In *Proceedings of the 23rd Design Automation Conference*, pages 454–460, 1986.

[Ros98] Wolfgang Rosenstiel. Rapid prototyping, emulation and hardware-software co-debugging. In *NATO ASI on System-Level Synthesis, Proceedings*, 1998.

[VG92] Frank Vahid and Daniel D. Gajski. Specification partitioning for system design. In *Proceedings of the 29th Design Automation Conference*, September 1992.

[VG95] Frank Vahid and Daniel D. Gajski. Incremental hardware estimation during hardware/software functional partitioning. *IEEE Transactions on VLSI Systems*, September 1995.

[VG99] Frank Vahid and Tony Givargis. The case for a Configure-and-Execute paradigm. In *Proceedings of the International Workshop on Hardware/Software Codesign*, 1999.

[VJL97] István Vassányi, István Jankovits, and Stefan Lenk. Datapath synthesis, communication processor design. Technical report, COPERNICUS Project, Intermediate Report, February 1997.

[Wir98] Niklaus Wirth. Hardware compilation: Translating programs into circuits. *IEEE Computer*, June 1998.

Index